the power of you

why you have the potential to change your life in an instant

ian lawton

Rational Spirituality Press

First published in 2014 by Rational Spirituality Press.
Second Edition 2016.

All enquiries to be directed to www.rspress.org.

A CIP catalogue record for this title is available from the British Library.

ISBN 978-0-9572573-9-9

Cover design by Ian Lawton.
Cover photograph by Kheng Guan Toh, licensed by dreamstime.com.
Author photograph by Simon Howson-Green.

this book has one object
and one object alone

it is to help you remember just how
powerful and in control you are

however much you may have been led
to believe the opposite

contents

preface

The power of 'mind over matter' is legendary. Anecdotal evidence of apparently superhuman strength – a mother lifting a car to save a trapped child, for example – abound.

In March 2014 a BBC *Horizon* documentary entitled 'The Power of the Placebo' reported how several enterprising health professionals have been pushing the boundaries of research into the power of the mind. For example in the UK sports psychologist Dr Chris Beedie of Aberystwyth University gave a number of professional track cyclists a supposedly legal, performance-enhancing pill that actually contained nothing more than cornflower. Although all of them were tired from an initial control run without the pill, every single cyclist recorded a faster time after taking the placebo. One even recorded a personal best.

In the US neurosurgeon Dr David Kallmes of the Mayo Clinic in Minnesota pioneered the technique of injecting liquid cement into damaged vertebrae, but then noticed that a small number of patients reported reduced pain and improvements in mobility even when the *wrong* vertebra had been treated. Going out on a limb he managed to conduct a study in which some patients were only given a placebo operation under local anaesthetic, although this mirrored the real thing as closely as possible. He found there was no statistical difference in the reported improvements between those who had the real operation and those who only experienced the placebo.

Also in the US more general research into the linkages between mind and matter has been expanding rapidly for several decades and is producing significant results. Leading the charge is former medical school professor and research scientist Dr Bruce Lipton, whose *Biology of Belief* is the seminal work in this area.

But perhaps you think such mind power can only be tapped into *in extremis*, or that it's something only some people can use, not you? Well, I've got news for you. *All* of us are using the power of our minds to manipulate the physical environment that forms our experience of life *all of the time*. For better or worse we never stop, even when we're asleep.

You don't have to take my word for it. The idea that we 'create' or 'manifest' our reality using the 'law of attraction' has formed the basis of many esoteric teachings, although often couched in obscure language to protect the authors from persecution by dominant orthodox religions. But the 'New Thought' movement that emerged in the nineteenth century can probably be credited as the first to openly discuss it, and when Wallace Wattles' seminal *The Science of Getting Rich* was published in 1910 it was a fully formed prototype for the plethora of modern books on the power of positive thinking, manifestation and attraction. Another landmark contribution was Napoleon Hill's *Think and Grow Rich*, which came out in 1937.

So what's different about *The Power of You*? Why do we need yet another tome? There are five main reasons.

First, for all that they've achieved some wonderful results for thousands of people, many of those who've read popular books such as Rhonda Byrne's *The Secret* have found themselves unable to put its theory into practice anywhere near as much as they'd have liked. Some may even have felt themselves to be complete failures as a result, thereby ending up in a worse emotional and psychological state than when they began. This is because, although the ideas themselves are extremely simple, putting them into practice in a widespread and consistent manner is *not* – at least not for many people – and anyone who pretends otherwise is perhaps presenting an unrealistic and potentially damaging panacea. So we need to make sure that we understand the reasons why *proactive*, *deliberate* or *conscious* creation of specific outcomes can be difficult. My own personal experiences of apparent 'failure' to create the life I desire have taken me to some pretty dark places, even quite recently, and I'll bring them into play where appropriate. The result is, I hope, a book that's grounded and realistic.

Second, although many contemporary spiritual writers have thrown their weight behind the law of attraction, few if any have been able to coherently slot it into the context of a broader worldview. For example, huge numbers of modern seekers believe in concepts such as reincarnation, karma, and life plans and contracts. So how does having supposedly complete free will to direct our experience fit into such a picture? Are there any restrictions on our free will, and if so what are they? Or do we need to develop a radically different model of how soul consciousness operates that brings everything together in a simple, coherent whole? There are no prizes for guessing my answer.

Third, this book has a fundamentally different emphasis from many others. This is because it's at least as much about *not* giving your power away, *not* avoiding responsibility by blaming other people, past lives, karma or life plans, and *not* attracting the things into your life that you *don't* want, as it's about proactively attracting those things you *do* want. This may sound somewhat heretical to those who've been schooled, quite correctly, that we shouldn't concentrate on negative outcomes, even if our focus is on their avoidance. But what I'm talking about are techniques for reducing the amount of time we spend thinking limiting thoughts, and I'd suggest these are at least as important as those used to attract specific outcomes.

Fourth, some people have a serious aversion to books on the law of attraction, and to the concept generally, not just because it may be difficult to put into practice. They see it as an idea that only well-off people in developed countries can afford to indulge, while it's of little use to those dying of starvation in Third World countries. They see nice people who get seriously ill, who maybe even die well before old age, and wonder how the law of attraction applies *there*. Perhaps more than anything they see books that are deliberately marketed to the masses who want to have more money, lose weight and so on, and they conclude that the conscious creation of abundance is self-centred, materialistic, and can only be obtained at the expense of others. These objections usually mean the baby is thrown out with the bathwater. Indeed they act as hugely significant blockages to the widespread acceptance of the idea that we have complete responsibility for creating our experience of the physical world – primarily as individuals but also, as a result, as a collective. Yet such acceptance is probably essential to the further evolution of the human race. Because these objections are *so* important, yet rarely if ever tackled properly, we'll cover them all in the opening chapter.

The fifth difference in this book is that, as far as I'm aware, no one has yet pulled together the wonderfully wise and consistent messages from the sources on which it's mainly based. In fact it seems to have been overlooked that, if the vast majority of the most celebrated channels of the last fifty years have *one consistent message* for us, it's that it's time for us to forsake childish religious restrictions and other unduly limiting spiritual ideas, to regain responsibility for and control of our lives, and to remember just how powerful we are as 'creator gods'. In fact the inference seems to be that this lies at the very heart of the shift in consciousness humanity is now witnessing.

If your life is already completely fulfilling and pleasurable because you're able to achieve such a state naturally and automatically, without the help of this or any other book, that's genuinely terrific – although of course we should never become too complacent, because life can change, sometimes dramatically, for *any* of us at *any* time. But in any case the vast majority of us probably feel there are at least *some* areas of our life that could do with *some* improvement.

You can read this book in only a few hours, although you'll probably want to revisit some of it, maybe repeatedly. Yet even after one read you should be better equipped to begin consciously and wilfully fashioning your experience of this world so that it's much more to your liking.

So how did *The Power of You* come about? Towards the end of 2013 I published the first edition of the first volume in this series, *Supersoul*, my first proper research book for some years. In this I'd talked about how we can start with a 'clean sheet' at any moment by invoking the 'law of grace' over the 'law of karma'. I'd also described a model in which time isn't continuous as we perceive it, but is in fact a 'discrete series of now-moments'. What I'd failed to do was put these two statements together.

In fact in both I'd waffled on about how invoking the law of grace wouldn't be easily done, how anyone attempting it would have to have total belief in what they were doing, and how they'd probably have to be a soul who'd already put the 'hard yards' in because there are 'no free lunches'. Each time as I was writing I'd known inside I was missing something important. I just couldn't put my finger on it.

Then, when *Supersoul* had been out for only about a month, several of my friends mentioned two channelled sources I'd not encountered before – Bashar and Elias, of whom more shortly. The following day I was reading through some of their material on-line and there they both were suggesting that, at least *theoretically*, in each now-moment we're creating our reality *entirely afresh* – except we normally allow past associations and experience to smother this process. That's when it finally hit me that so many of us have been working from a spiritual worldview based on past-life karma, life plans and so on that is, arguably, profoundly misleading – and no longer serves us as we move into a new era of human consciousness.

In fact I had severe doubts about the concept of karma as long ago as 2004 when I wrote the original *Book of the Soul* – this coupled with a longstanding distrust of any worldview that suggested humanity is anything other than in charge of its own destiny. But even as someone attempting a close study of the subject it took me an age to recognise that karma was probably a seriously unhelpful concept. Nevertheless four years later, in the revised *Big Book of the Soul*, I proposed that we should 'forget karma, experience is all that matters'. What's more it's now clear to me that *any* suggestion that there's any sort of karmic law whereby events of the apparent 'past' can *definitively* dictate what is happening to us now is not only profoundly misleading but also limiting, even damaging.

Let's make sure we understand this, because it's immensely important. *If* one were to see the laws of karma and of attraction as synonymous, and as describing the way the attitudes and beliefs we hold in each moment of now exert an attraction that creates the reality we experience in what appears to be our 'future', then that's fine and helpful. The problem is that most people assume that this process *must* also be applied in reverse, so that at least to some extent our 'now' is the result of past thoughts and actions. But it doesn't *have* to be.

Of course, if you *believe* that the 'past' *must* influence your current experience, it absolutely will. In fact we've evolved to use 'inductive reasoning' whereby past associations inform the judgments we make in the now – it helped when we were constantly under threat from woolly mammoths, sabre-toothed tigers and other predators, and it still helps us to learn to avoid all sorts of different dangers in the modern world. But we can afford to start rewiring our brains, if we *choose* to, so that undesirable 'past' experiences that have formed into limiting beliefs no longer *have* to dictate what we believe and how we act in the now. For most of us this can take time and we may never, while in human form, achieve the perfection of removing limiting thoughts completely. But, at least theoretically, if our ability to discipline our thoughts matched our certain knowledge of the workings of time and of the law of attraction, we could literally start with a clean sheet in each or any new moment of now, and immediately create an entirely different experience for ourselves. Hence the subtitle 'why you have the *potential* to change your life *in an instant*'.

This realisation was what triggered me to think there was perhaps another book to be written. That's when further research revealed that nearly every major contemporary source of channelled wisdom has focused to a significant extent on the idea that we create our own reality, and that we should learn to take more deliberate and conscious control of this process. I also realised that this supreme cross-source consistency had perhaps been somewhat overlooked. For me that sealed the deal, and *The Power of You* was born.

But that wasn't all. In the original edition of *Supersoul* I'd developed various models of supersoul consciousness, but I'd been unable to choose between them. Now things were starting to become clearer and I immediately started work on a thorough revision to the relevant chapters, the new model being based on the triple concepts of the supersoul, of simultaneous lives, and of the law of attraction. Having said that its implications turned out to be rather more dramatic and far-reaching than even I'd anticipated when I gave *Supersoul* the subtitle 'a radical worldview for a new consciousness', and I must admit to baulking at them myself on more than one occasion.

As I intimated earlier, this new model of how consciousness operates is potentially the first to seamlessly accommodate the idea that each of us has complete free will to direct our own experience for ourselves. The full details are of course in the revised edition of *Supersoul*, but here are the summarised 'ten principles' that emerge from it:

1. We are holographic, expeditionary projections sent out by a supersoul consciousness possessing a wisdom and power of divine proportions. Myriad supersouls are involved in the simulation game we call 'human life on earth', which is just one of myriad different realities they project aspects of themselves into.

2. After death we continue to identify with the personality of the life we just left, so this and the individual 'soul' are the same consciousness.

3. Although we're engaged in the expansion of consciousness, we don't develop in a linear fashion as we move from one reincarnatory life to another. Instead the lives of all souls projected by the supersoul are happening at the same time – even if they're operating in different human eras.

4. ‘My’ many lives means nothing unless we’re genuinely adopting our supersoul level of consciousness, which involves appreciating that we’re far more powerful and multi-faceted than we normally recognise. Any experiences we have of ‘past’ or ‘future’ lives are most likely those of other ‘resonant souls’ projected by our supersoul with whom we have an especially close connection – for example because of strongly shared traits or challenges, or because they act as contrasts.

5. Each of us is fundamentally responsible for creating our own experience in each moment of now. We are not limited by ‘past karma’, whether from this life or a supposedly previous one, unless we believe we are. Nor will other resonant souls tend to be able to exert a strongly disruptive influence over us unless we believe they can and choose to let them.

6. Our supersoul chooses our ‘birth givens’, and these vary considerably. They include our own sex, our main psychological and physical traits and propensities – in terms of both challenges and strengths – and the ethnicity, socio-economic position and geographical location of our parents. On that basis we’re here to ‘paint the best picture we can with the palette we’ve been given’. Other than that any pre-birth planning of events in our adult lives, or ‘soul contracts’ with others, are probably kept to a minimum to give us maximum free will to direct our experience. It is also unlikely that most of us have a preplanned ‘life purpose’, because again this would tend to detract from our free will to follow whatever purpose we desire – and to change that purpose, should we so choose, at any time.

7. Angels and guides may well be other aspects of our own supersoul, and they won’t tend to interfere with our experience on the basis that they supposedly ‘know best’ and ‘want to keep us on our path’. Usually therefore

synchronicities will only represent the sophisticated underlying dynamics of how our *own* creation and attraction process crystallises into our experience.

8. Having said that, insights and guidance are always available if we *proactively* ask for them, or if we *attract* them to ourselves automatically by our conscious intentions and actions. Such guidance might come, for example, from wiser, non-incarnate aspects of our supersoul, or from other resonant souls – perhaps even operating in the 'future' – who have overcome similar challenges. By the same token we can provide guidance to them by overcoming our own challenges, if they're open to it.

9. On rare occasions we might make a new agreement with our supersoul, at a subconscious level, to take on a new challenge in our adult lives. But it's always best to take responsibility for any challenge by assuming you created or attracted it, or at least by knowing you control your reaction to it. Any tendency to ascribe challenges to 'past' karma, life plans or soul contracts can lead to an abrogation of responsibility for what we're creating in the now, and detract from our extensive power to turn any situation around.

10. Under the supersoul model *everything* can be seen as altruistic, because everything that each soul experiences is designed to add to the databanks of the parent consciousness. Any particularly challenging circumstances or birth givens can best be seen in the context of 'taking one for the team', and each of us can be characterised as a 'lead representative of team supersoul gaining experience at the coalface of space-time on behalf of the collective'.

A significant portion of this book takes the form of channelled material, about which anyone can reasonably express some doubt.

This especially in an age where huge numbers of people are attempting the process, not always with any great understanding of what they're doing. As the great Qabalist Dion Fortune once observed in the introduction to her *Cosmic Doctrine*: 'A spirit communication may come from a perfectly genuine spirit, and yet be valueless. Even if a man survives bodily death, dying is not going to cure him of being a fool... If you set your front door open, the kind of person who would come walking in would be more likely to steal the umbrellas from the hall than undertake to instruct you in profound spiritual truths; and so it is with psychism.'

Period	*Source*	*Channel*
57-79	Pathwork Guide	Eva Pierrakos
63-84	Seth	Jane Roberts
79-	Ramtha	JZ Knight
83-	Bashar	Darryl Anka
88-	Abraham (a plural entity)	Esther Hicks
91-05	'God'	Neale Donald Walsch
94-97	The Way of Mastery (Jeshua-Jesus)	Jayem (Jon Marc Hammer)
95-	Elias	Mary Ennis

Nevertheless I'm prepared to assert that the profundity and wisdom consistently found in the sources we'll be using makes it extremely unlikely that we're dealing with either misguided spirits or merely human musings. They are listed in the table above, along with the names of their human channels, ordered according to the period over which the material was produced. I haven't included a detailed background on each source because they've been deliberately chosen as some of the best-known of the modern era, but more information is easily available on-line or using the references listed under 'Channelled Sources' at the end. This latter includes an explanation of the reasoning behind the specific texts

I've used.

However a couple of linkages are worth pointing out, apart from the obvious fact that they all concentrate on the idea that we create our own reality. First the most recent source, Elias, appears to have a reasonable acquaintance with the Seth material – although the two sets are by no means identical, and different phraseology and terminology is often used. Second, in *The Way of Mastery* trilogy – comprising *The Way of the Heart, The Way of Transformation* and *The Way of Knowing* – Jeshua-Jesus makes several references to also being the author of the earlier, renowned *Course in Miracles*, which according to its channel Helen Shucman did indeed come from Jesus. But, while *The Way of Mastery* repeatedly emphasises our role in manifesting our reality, rather less explicit stress is placed on this in *A Course in Miracles*. What's more the language and terminology of the latter is somewhat more stilted and Christianised than the former. For these reasons I've used *The Way of Mastery* trilogy as a prime source in this book, even though generally speaking many of the messages are common to both.

The only other point to make is that I'm not aware of any major earlier source that concentrates on creation, manifestation and attraction in the way these do. This makes the late 50s the earliest point at which this shift in emphasis in channelled material seems to commence.

Once you fully take on board that you're decidedly *not* a victim of anyone else in your life, or of any 'past' karma, or of any unalterable life plan, there are no longer *any* hiding places or excuses. The *responsibility* conferred by the understanding that we create everything we experience at some level of our consciousness is massive, and will undoubtedly prove too much for some at this time. But that doesn't mean a more realistic and sophisticated view shouldn't be made available so that those who *are* ready can let go of the relatively simplistic and limiting beliefs many of us have clung onto until now. None more so than me.

The revised edition of *Supersoul* includes an appendix in which I've attempted to apply the new model to various aspects of my own experience, including the 'dark night of the soul' I experienced in 2011-12 – which I now interpret quite differently. In particular, repeatedly during that time I would wonder if the ever-increasing challenges were all part of my life plan, and whether I was 'suffering so I could grow', and so on and so forth. If I'd known then what I know now I'd have taken much more responsibility, and looked much harder, much sooner for the attitudes and beliefs that undoubtedly played the greatest role in my misery. In short I've little doubt now that I'd have discovered my inner victim far sooner than I actually did. So I know from hard personal experience that ideas like life plans and soul contracts can give people excuses to stay stuck where they are instead of taking full responsibility for their experience *in the now*.

What's more, the message of this book isn't *just* one of responsibility. It also makes it clear that mastering the human experience isn't a walk in the park, and that we can take real *credit* for challenges we successfully overcome; that we have real *freedom* to direct our experience wherever we want it to go; most important, that we all possess a supreme creative *power*, if only we choose to recognise this fact and use it.

The following quote from the inimitable Seth pretty much sums up what it's about:

> If you find yourself assailed by physical difficulties, however, you begin to wonder what is wrong. Sometimes you blame others, your own background, or a previous life – if you accept reincarnation. You may hold God or the devil responsible, or you may simply say, 'That is life,' and accept the negative experience as a necessary portion of your lot. You may finally come to a half-understanding of the nature of reality and wail, 'I believe that I have caused these ill effects, but I find myself unable to reverse them.' If this is the case, then regardless of what you have told yourself thus far, you still do not believe that you are the creator of

> your own experience. As soon as you recognize this fact you can begin at once to alter those conditions that cause you dismay or dissatisfaction.
>
> If you are in poor health, you can remedy it. If your personal relationships are unsatisfactory, you can change them for the better. If you are in poverty, you can instead find yourself surrounded by abundance… If you were born poor, or born sick, then it certainly seems to you that these circumstances were thrust upon you. Yet they were not, and to some extent or another they can be changed for the better. This does *not* mean that effort is not required, and determination. It *does* mean that you are not powerless to change events and that each of you, regardless of your position, status, circumstances or physical condition, is in control of your own personal experience. (Seth, *NPR*, Preface)

Before we begin in earnest, a few more detailed preliminaries. I use the word 'chapter' to refer to each main heading, and 'section' for each sub-heading. The 'key quotes' at the end of each section are in alphabetical order of source. Abbreviations are used for the names of books whose full details can be found under 'Channelled Sources' at the end. For non-book sources, dates or names are given that can be mapped to the web resources listed in the same place. Any italics in quotes are original; comments in square brackets are mine, for clarification; and ellipses are used to indicate the omission of intervening words, sentences or paragraphs that are repetitive or irrelevant.

Occasionally different pieces of advice in the quotes may seem to contradict each other, and where I've spotted this I've tried to explain why. It's usually because they fit different situations, so follow what resonates for you in the moment. On another day during a reread another piece of advice may be more relevant.

But generally speaking please remember this isn't intended to be a detailed self-help book. Its primary aim is to prove the *theory* of our responsibility for and freedom to create our own reality, and the various ramifications of that. Of course it does provide *some* practical advice. But I'd expect that, once the fundamental *idea* has been fully accepted, readers will either turn to the original sources themselves, or to the suggested further reading provided at the end, or to any number of the myriad self-help books based on this topic, for detailed advice about how to really put the theory into *practice*. Or, for those who're already well informed about the topic, its aim is to provide a fuller and broader theoretical context, alongside detailed cross-source confirmation of the various ideas.

Finally, a few thankyous are in order: to Lorna Franklin and Juliet Vorster for their constructive and illuminating feedback on the manuscript; and to Simon Howson-Green, Elena Adams and Stephen Gawtry for their invaluable assistance with marketing. But my greatest thanks must be reserved for the sources themselves, for their profound wisdom; and for their respective channels, for their dedication in receiving and recording the messages, and for 'getting out of the way'. Surely only the most ardent sceptic would be prepared to suggest that the words you'll find quoted here are merely those of ordinary human consciousnesses.

Ian Lawton
May 2014

even if your greater self chooses
certain circumstances in your life...

you still create your
reaction to them

I indicated in the Preface that I'd begin by facing, head-on, the most obvious objections to the idea that we create our own reality.

I have every sympathy for those who are sceptical of the extent of our control over our lives. What they see as obvious exceptions – such as those born into abject poverty, or nice people who become seriously ill or even die prematurely – are nearly always ignored in a body of literature that can sometimes seem somewhat relentlessly upbeat and, perhaps, unrealistic. Yet for many people the exceptions disprove the rule to such an extent that they conclude we can't be controlling our reality *at all*.

I cannot hope to understand, let alone explain, the full intricacies of these apparent exceptions, which are somewhat ignored even by our channelled sources themselves. But even to try is hugely important if the idea that we create our own reality is going to become persuasive to whole new sections of society – especially perhaps to those who naturally tend towards a highly unselfish, caring and altruistic perspective.

One of their concerns is, of course, that creating abundance for ourselves means others have to lose out. This objection doesn't fit within this chapter and will be covered later. But, as to the rest, here we go...

DO ADVERSE BIRTH CIRCUMSTANCES LIMIT OUR ABILITY TO CREATE?

We all know that people born into a financially secure and loving environment can and often do go off the rails, while there are many notable examples of people born into poor and disadvantaged families who have gone on to achieve amazing things, all down to their own hard work and determination.

But can we really say that someone born into abject poverty, or who was so unwanted they spent their entire childhood being shifted from one care home to another – possibly on the receiving end of all manner of abuse – is just as in control of their own destiny as those of us who enjoyed a far better start in life? What about children born into starvation-level poverty in the Third World? Does it not seem a little blasé and self-satisfied to suggest we all have equal access to abundance?

In the Preface I indicated that each of us is quite clearly subject to a set of birth givens that include our own sex, our main psychological and physical traits and propensities – in terms of both challenges and strengths – and the ethnicity, socio-economic position and geographical location of our parents. It's equally clear that these givens can vary enormously from one person to another. On the basis that the lives of all the supersoul's probes are happening at the same time – something our sources will confirm in due course – I contend that they're not chosen by an individual soul that reincarnates in one life after another, each time selecting new challenges based on what's gone before. Instead they're chosen by the supersoul itself as a unique set of traits and circumstances, because it's constantly looking for different ways to express itself and to expand. On that basis any person with a very challenging set of birth givens – for example being born in an area of the globe ravaged by war or famine, or with severe disabilities of some sort – can be seen as 'taking one for the team', but even this can be seen as a deliberate choice by another, higher level of their *own* consciousness.

That aside, on a prosaic level one could argue that, generally speaking, a person born into extreme poverty will find it practically harder to create a life of *financial* abundance than another who's not so disadvantaged. Nevertheless I'm sure no one would argue that this would be in any sense *impossible*. Indeed, as we'll see, if said person were to fully understand the rules of the law of attraction then at least *theoretically* it should be no harder for them to create financial abundance than anyone else.

What's more it may be that their life has other compensations. For example, we all know that many cultures in poorer parts of the world have a far greater sense of family and community than in the supposedly developed world, despite sometimes abject poverty. They often have smiles on their faces and are ready to share what little they have with a stranger. Can anyone dare to suggest this is somehow a less rewarding or valid life experience than one of financial abundance that's entirely lacking in love and compassion? We also know just how much those who're in some way less able – paralympians, for example – can be shining examples to the rest of us as to just what's possible when someone has the requisite attitude and belief. If that's not creating their own reality to maximum expansive effect under apparently difficult circumstances, I don't know what is.

To sum up, our sources agree that there are very good reasons why our supersoul might choose what appear in human terms to be adverse birth circumstances. They also make it clear in this and later sections that, however difficult the circumstances we face, we're entirely in control of our *reaction* to them – in terms of whether we overcome the challenges or allow them to defeat us.

key quotes

Do you know why you are the identity you are now? Because you have been most of the other roles before and now you are experiencing this one. Why weren't you born a starving child rather than the opulent entity that you are? Because you have been the starving child who wanted to be the opulent entity, and so you are... The wonderful thing about this kingdom is that it is ongoing and changeable, and you can be any player you wish to be. And as you advance upon the platform of life, you advance to plateaus which offer you a stage to play out the illusions that will provide the greatest learning within your being. And upon that stage you have the freedom to become king or pauper, lover or loved, slave or freedman, whatever illusion will provide you the understanding your soul is needing for fulfillment. (Ramtha, *WB*, chapter 16)

Suppose the worst, that in this life you have the following background: you are poor, you are of a minority race, you are not intellectual... you have a serious physical defect and you are no beauty. Now you set these challenges for yourself... This does not mean that you cannot use all of your courage and resolution to solve these problems. You set them in the hope that you *will* solve them. You did not set them like millstones about your neck, hoping ahead of time that you would drown. (Seth, *SS*, Appendix)

Challenges [are set up] by the whole self... At the same 'time' so to speak, that this personality is born into a minority race, in a completely different era it may be born rich, secure and aristocratic. It [the whole self] is searching out different methods of experience and expansion. (Seth, *SS*, Appendix)

If you were born poor, or born sick, then it certainly seems to you that these circumstances were thrust upon you. Yet they were not, and to some extent or another they can be changed for the better. This does *not* mean that effort is not required, and determination. It *does* mean that you are not powerless to change events and that each of you, regardless of your position, status, circumstances or physical condition, is in control of your own personal experience. (Seth, *NPR*, Preface)

If you have decided upon a situation in which a critical organic lack or disability is involved, and are born with a severe disease, for example, than that is the context in which you will experience this particular focus in corporeal reality. There will be a reason for it, and that reason will lie in those abilities that you have left free and open for you to pursue... Within the bounds of creaturehood certain things are possible and certain things are not. You cannot regenerate a limb, or grow a new one. You can cure yourself of an 'incurable' disease if you realize that your point of power is in the present... The main point is not to concentrate upon the liabilities but to pursue those abilities that you have... Often, particularly in the case of mental or physical birth defects, the incapacitated person will be accepting that role not only because of personal reasons; he or she will also be choosing that part for the family as a whole. (Seth, *NPR*, chapter 19)

A person may choose a great talent instead, through which he or she will perceive reality and concentrate all experience. This will serve as a formidable focus, yet by its nature it may often preclude other experiences that many individuals find quite normal. (Seth, *NPR*, chapter 19)

Your potential *is* unlimited in all that you've chosen to do. Do not assume that a soul which has incarnated in a body which you call limited has not reached its full potential, for you do not know what that soul was *trying to do*. You do not understand its agenda. You are unclear as to its *intent*. (Walsch, *CWG I*, chapter 1)

You choose everything. Your parents. Your country of birth. All the circumstances surrounding your re-entry. Similarly, throughout the days and times of your life you continue to choose and to create people, events and circumstances designed to bring you the exact, right, and perfect opportunities you now desire in order to know yourself as you *truly* are. In other words, no one is 'disadvantaged', given what the soul wishes to accomplish. For example, the soul may *wish* to work with a handicapped body or in a repressive society or under enormous political or economic constraints, in order to produce the conditions needed to accomplish what it has set out to do. So we see that people do face 'disadvantages' in the *physical* sense, but that these are actually the right and perfect conditions *metaphysically*. (Walsch, *CWG II*, chapter 12)

DO WE HAVE LIFE PLANS THAT CAN OVERRIDE OUR FREE WILL?

Most contemporary worldviews based on reincarnation make the assumption that we plan our lives before birth in order to present ourselves with the challenges that we need to grow. What's more, such planning is not thought to be limited to our birth givens as discussed in the previous section, but is assumed to extend into our adult lives too.

Such a worldview has always been somewhat at odds with the

idea that we have complete free will to create our life in whatever way we choose from moment to moment. Up to now commentators like me have attempted to explain this contradiction away by asserting that such planning includes only major probabilities and lesser possibilities, and that free will can override any of these. However we've also confused the picture by suggesting that we have guides who're wiser than us, and who attempt to keep us on our 'life path' because they know best what's good for us.

As indicated in the Preface, our new model dispenses with these assumptions. Instead it suggests that, apart from our obvious birth givens, life planning is unlikely to extend into our adult lives – precisely so that the individual soul probe has complete free will to 'paint the best picture they can from the palette they've been given'. Arguably this is exactly why so many people are able to completely reverse apparently advantageous or adverse birth circumstances. Our sources confirm this view and insist that, at least once we're no longer under the control of our parents or other guardians, *nothing* overrides our free will. I should note that there are some *possible* exceptions to this that we'll consider in the next section, although these still don't contravene the law of attraction.

key quotes

You are not a puppet acting out that which has been intended before. You have the choice, in every moment, to decide what is most appropriate from your ever-evolving perspective, *for you have grown beyond that which you were as you emerged into this body – for this life experience has already added unto that perspective.* (Abraham, *LOA*, part 5)

The reason you do not consciously know what [your] specific goals are is because there were no specific goals. You had, before your physical birth, general intentions, such as being happy, being an uplifter, having continuing growth – but the specific processes or vehicles through which you will achieve any of those things is up to you to decide here and now. In this time, you are the creator. (Abraham, *LOA*, part 5)

You choose where you are wishing to be entering physical focus, at which time period, at which season, with which parents, and with the knowledge of the probabilities of other family members. (Elias, 11 May 97)

In *no* circumstance is there anything of creation that has the power to dictate to you the choice that you will make. (Jeshua, *WOH*, lesson 2)

You had a hand in the development of your childhood environment. You chose the circumstances. This does not mean you are at the mercy of those circumstances. It means that you set challenges to be overcome, set goals to be reached, set up frameworks of experience through which you could develop, understand and fulfill certain abilities. The creative power to form your experience is within you now, as it has been since the time of your birth and before. You may have chosen a particular theme for this existence, a certain framework of conditions, but within these you have the freedom to experiment, create, and alter conditions and events. (Seth, *NPR*, chapter 2)

The purpose is to create your experience – and thus create your *self* – in the glorious moment of now. You do not, therefore, choose the life you will experience ahead of time. You may, however, select the persons, places, and events – the conditions and circumstances, the challenges and obstacles, the opportunities and options – with which to create your experience. You may select the colors for your palette, the tools for your chest, the machinery for your shop. What you create with these is your business. (Walsch, *CWG I*, chapter 1)

WHY DO NICE PEOPLE GET ILL OR DIE EARLY?

The whole issue of nice people suffering serious illness, or becoming physically or mentally challenged in an accident, or even dying prematurely, is perhaps the greatest reason why the law of attraction is not accepted as universal – and is often rejected in its entirety. Most of us will have seen an example of this in our own lives at some point or another, and by 'nice' we tend to mean those who're kind, positive in outlook and unselfish. Given that we don't accept the idea that some sort of capricious old man with a beard sits atop fluffy clouds making irrational decisions about such things, any more than we accept that anything happens by pure chance alone, what *is* going on here?

We'll see in a later chapter that our sources insist that our health is conditioned by our beliefs about and attitudes to it, and is self-created. So the first thing we must accept is that we *never* really know what's going on in someone else's mind, however much we think we understand them. What's more we all know that outward appearances can be deceptive. So we should appreciate that often it's our own sense of loss or of righteous indignation that means we refuse to accept that someone we saw in one light could *possibly* have attracted a major illness or even premature death by their *own* attitudes and beliefs. Perhaps even worse, if it's *you* that's been affected yourself, how many of us have the searing honesty and desire for truth to go deep within and see where our *own* attitudes and beliefs could possibly have been the cause of our illness or accident?

If this sounds unduly harsh and inhumane, let's bring a little context to the table. Our sources tell us that human life is effectively a game – albeit an important and extremely useful one to the expansion of consciousness – which is much easier to play if you know the rules and don't become too trapped in its manifold illusions. Many of you will have heard of the essentially Buddhist idea of cultivating 'nonattachment', so that we can lose possessions and even people we love dearly without our whole life falling apart. On top of that this whole worldview is one in which there's no 'death', only consciousness that's forever expanding in new and ingenious ways and in different environments. So even if we do manage to create – or more accurately unconsciously attract – a major illness, accident or even untimely death, and however painful this may be to ourselves and others in human form, from our supersoul perspective it's just a drop in the ocean and another rich part of the tapestry of experience.

One fascinating and highly relevant case in point is that of Jane Roberts herself, the woman who channelled Seth for more than twenty years. For the two years up to her death she was bedridden with extreme rheumatoid arthritis, just as her mother had been when Jane was forced to look after her as a little girl. Seth insisted again and again that, although her disease was to some extent hereditary, she didn't *have* to accept it into her life and could have avoided it with different thinking, beliefs and behaviours. He also suggests that different people can project the same innermost conflict into entirely different areas of their lives – for example into poverty, loneliness or ill-health.

All of that having been said, is it possible that *some* major events in *some* people's adult lives don't just occur because they've attracted them in the ordinary course of events? Our sources are relatively silent on this issue, not least because they're not often asked the relevant questions. We can probably reject the idea of advance planning *before* birth because it appears there's constant feedback of experience to the supersoul – so that no life plan for adulthood could ever remain static and still relevant, but would be constantly changing. Indeed the whole process of consciousness growing and evolving is inherently, and probably hugely, dynamic.

But, rather than any event being preplanned as such, is it possible that sometimes we might make a *new agreement* with our supersoul to take on a new challenge? This would obviously be at a subconscious level, perhaps in our dream state, and one might still argue that we'd attracted it to the extent that we'd shown ourselves ready to take on such a challenge. Yet this time what might appear to be an adverse event would have an expansionary underlying dynamic rather than the normal limiting one. What's more, as usual the person who took on the new challenge would be completely in control of how they reacted to it.

Once more paralympians are a good example. Of course some have been challenged since birth, but when someone faces a new and significant challenge in their adult life – whether by accident or illness – they face a major choice. They can sink under the weight of self-pity, or rise up and become a shining example. Huge numbers of paralympians have chosen the latter course, and I can't help but have an inner intuition that *for some at least* their accident or illness was a new challenge agreed on a subconscious level with their supersoul, rather than self-created by limiting beliefs and attitudes.

The same will almost certainly be true of *some* people who agree to contract a serious disease such as cancer, not only as a challenge for themselves, but to have the chance to act as an example of the power of belief and of fighting spirit to others too. Or, if premature death is the chosen path for whatever reason, the example for others may be one of calm and loving acceptance. All these are, again, instances of taking one for the team so that the consciousness of the entire supersoul is expanded and enhanced. If any of this occurs with a relatively young person, say in their teens, this can be even more powerful – even if also ostensibly more distressing.

While we'll see at the end of this chapter that our sources advise we should always see our life experiences as attracted or created by ourselves, and generally they don't support the idea of static life plans, a few of them seem to at least hint that apparently adverse events in our adult lives may be deliberately 'chosen' because they have a silver lining – although they don't explain exactly how or by who. But Jeshua in particular goes further and describes how this can be a new challenge that at a deeper level we've agreed to take on – and have attracted *not* through limiting beliefs and attitudes but because we've already demonstrated our capacity to overcome, and to turn a potential trial into a gift.

Does our attracting a new challenge in this way contravene our free will, in as much as we only agree to it at a non-conscious level? Perhaps, perhaps not. What we can say is that in any case our new supersoul model tends to move us more towards seeing our lives as altruistically lived for the benefit of the collective rather than just of ourselves as an individual, so perhaps in such a context this becomes an unimportant question. What we can also say definitively again is that such a decision is made at a higher level of our *own* consciousness, that of our supersoul, rather than imposed on us from outside.

key quotes

It is quite true that you may be calling a calamity to yourself because you, as a soul, are ready to discover a greater depth of love and forgiveness in yourself. Life might bring you challenges, but only because you have asked it to bring you challenges so that you can grow your capacity to maturely direct love in this world. *Nothing can occur that you have not called to yourself*. (Jeshua, *WOK*, lesson 4)

In much of your so-called new age movement there is much judgment, *much judgment*, much abhorrence of anything that does not look like manifesting wealth, having perfectly curved hips, and a multitude of loving friends. That is a naïve attitude. (Jeshua, *WOK*, lesson 11)

Each individual has what I will call a psychic territory of power. This represents an inviolate area in which the person insists upon remaining supreme, aware of his or her uniqueness and abilities. This psychic region will be protected at all costs, and here there is indeed immunity from all disease or lack... Because of different personal characteristics, one individual will hold qualities of the mind, say, inviolate, and work out challenges through bodily illness. Another may choose the severest poverty projecting into that situation his or her own unresolved conflicts. Another may choose alcoholism. (Seth, *NPR*, chapter 17)

[Referring to how birth challenges can be chosen to test the whole family] The same applies to seeming tragedies such as accidents, or severe illnesses that come at any time. (Seth, *NPR*, chapter 19)

There is *no* coincidence, and *nothing* happens 'by accident'. Each event and adventure is called *to* your self *by* your self in order that you might create and experience who you really are. All true Masters know this. That is why mystic Masters remain unperturbed in the face of the worst experiences of life – as *you* would define them. (Walsch, *CWG I*, chapter 1)

ARE WE EVER HELPLESS VICTIMS, OR IS EVERYTHING OUR RESPONSIBILITY?

If we put the possible exceptions mentioned in the previous section to one side, our sources are adamant that we should recognise we create our reality from moment to moment. They understand that if we hit a major new challenge, or if we're in the depth of a depressive rut where nothing seems to be going right, then it's easy for us to deny responsibility and insist there's no way we could have *chosen* that. They understand that we then blame capricious gods, or blind chance, or life plans that involve the idea that we have to suffer in order to grow, or simply other people. They understand that we move into *victim mode*. What's more they know that nearly all of us do this to a greater or lesser extent at some point in our lives.

They also try to remind us, some gently, some less so, that all this is just a failure to accept the basic reality that we're entirely responsible for creating our *own* experience, and for our *reaction* to our birth givens and to any other events, circumstances or people we attract into our lives. There are considerably more quotes in this section than in any other, and some of them are quite lengthy. That's quite deliberate. Unless and until we're prepared to take *total* responsibility, the bulk of the advice in the rest of the book will fall on deaf ears.

key quotes

Nothing merely shows up in your experience. *You attract it – all of it. No exceptions*... People often explain, in the midst of unwanted things occurring in their experience, that they are certain *they* did not create such a thing... And while we know that you did not deliberately bring this unwanted thing into your experience, we must still explain that only *you* could have caused it, because no one else has the power to attract what comes to you but you. (Abraham, *LOA*, part 2)

No other creates in your experience. You are doing it all; you get all of the credit. As you observe your own life experience and the experiences of those around you, we want you to understand that there is not a shred of evidence that is contrary to these powerful Laws that we are expressing. (Abraham, *LOA*, part 3)

So you wonder... how you create your realities, or why you create your reality, or why you choose the experiences that you choose! Or perhaps, do you choose these experiences? You find it easier to be viewing all things as prearranged agreements. (Elias, 24 Jun 96)

You believe that there are certain experiences within your reality that are uncomfortable or distressful or what you deem to be negative that you do not create... If you are interacting with another individual, and you are experiencing conflict and you are experiencing what you identify as hurtfulness, you are not expressing to yourself that you are creating that within yourself. You are expressing to yourself that the other individual is creating an action which is thusly hurtful *to* you. If you are experiencing a dis-ease, you do not express to yourselves that you are creating this dis-ease. You express to yourself that you are being attacked by some element of physical origin that is creating the dis-ease. The dis-ease is creating itself, and it is 'infecting' you. If you are participating in what you term to be an accident and you are severing your leg, you express that this is an accident and that some physical object has severed your leg. You have not created that action, but it has occurred *to* you. You also believe that other individuals hold the power to be creating certain elements of your reality for you. This creates your perception of victim. You may be experiencing this role of victim in many, many different types of expressions. Now; I express to you, you create *all* of your reality. You create every moment of your reality – every breath, every thought, every emotion, every feeling, every action, every encounter. Every interaction of your reality – every circumstance and every 'thing' within your reality – is created by yourself. No other individual, no circumstance, no essence, no element of consciousness may be creating any aspect of your reality for you. This is an intrusive action, and consciousness and essences are not intrusive. This is an intrinsic quality of consciousness, to not be intrusive. Therefore, *no* element of your reality may be created by any other expression outside of yourself. Now; you create the illusion within your beliefs that outside influences create aspects of your reality, but in actuality, you *always* hold choices. (Elias, 17 Jun 00)

Each time an individual creates a response within their perception that they assess any aspect of their reality is being created *for* them and that they are not *choosing* that creation, the individual is automatically also expressing some identification and association with the aspect of victim... That role denies you all of your choices. (Elias, 13 Nov 2000)

Flatten the hill of beliefs that express to you that you may merely create some aspects of your reality but that other aspects of your reality are dictated to you by other individuals or situations or circumstances. Literally, it matters not what other individuals choose, for they are not creating your reality, they are not creating your perception, and they do not dictate to you what your choices may or shall be. (Elias, 31 Aug 01)

[The Way of Mastery] does not know the word avoidance. It does not know deception, manipulation or control. It does not know blame, although it watches these things arise as echoes of old patterns now outgrown. (Jeshua, *WOH*, lesson 1)

[Suggested affirmation] 'In each moment, regardless of what I believe I see, regardless of the feelings that arise within my awareness, I and I alone am wholly one hundred percent responsible for them. No one has caused them. No great force in the universe has made this perception well up within my consciousness. I have selected it... I am a creator of all that I think and see and experience. I am free always. Nothing impinges on me, but the thoughts I have chosen to hold within. Nothing imprisons me, but my own perception of imprisonment. Nothing limits me at any level or dimension of experience, save that which I have chosen.' (Jeshua, *WOH*, lesson 2)

Any time you react to what you believe is outside of yourself – you may be absolutely *positive* of this – you have elected to pick up that old pebble that says, 'I'm a victim of the world I see. What I experience is caused by forces outside of me. The fault really is in my mother, my brother, my father, my partner, my child. The fault really is in the government, and the planet, and the quality of air. The fault really is from a source outside of me, and I have no choice but to react to it.' To which I can only say: 'Would you rather be right, or happy?' (Jeshua, *WOH*, lesson 8)

The mind that chooses, in even a small part, to perceive itself as a *victim* of its world of experience, remains powerless. It remains in a state that generates frustration, weakness, fear, self-doubt, unworthiness, suffering, pain... separation from others and lack of fulfillment. (Jeshua, *WOH*, lesson 8)

You are free in this moment and in every moment to simply say: 'I think I will adopt the perspective of a master – no sense in blame, no sense in feeling like a victim. What I am experiencing is wholly mine. I must, therefore, have wanted it. (Jeshua, *WOK*, lesson 11)

We might share with you that victimization is one of the 'booby prizes' chosen pervasively by humanity – the victim game. Many are quite committed to seeing how well they can play it out. One could say that the victimization game has affected virtually every mind in the human domain. (Jeshua, *WOK*, lesson 11)

You still overlook the tremendous significance of what you create with your consciousness. And your being disconnected from it causes the real, the worst, suffering. There is no other suffering as acute as the one when you do not know that you have created what you experience... For if you do not know that you have created them, you will always feel helpless; you will always feel in the hands of a power which you cannot comprehend. This power is truly your own consciousness, my friends. (Pathwork, 2 Sep 69)

You are not a helpless pawn in anyone's hands. This is the important question, the all-important fact of life that truly alters your entire self-perception and attitude toward living. Not knowing this will make you constantly feel victimized by circumstances beyond your control... It requires a great deal of honesty, discipline, the overcoming of resistance until an individual can make this all-important 'switch' within his entire approach to life, from feeling himself helpless to seeing his own creations in all respects. (Pathwork, 2 Sep 69)

Great creative God that you are, who do you think has created your life? Do you believe that a supreme being or forces outside of you have controlled your life?.. All you have ever done, been, or experienced, you are wholly responsible for. You, who have the power to create the magnificence of stars, have created every moment and every circumstance of your life. Who you are, you chose to be. What you look like, you created. How you live, you wholly designed and destined. That is the exercise and privilege, if you will, of being God/man... Do you think that things happen to you simply by chance?.. There is no such thing as an accident or a coincidence in this kingdom. And no one is a victim of anyone else's will or designs. Everything that happens to you, you have thought and felt into your life. Either it has been fantasized in what-ifs or in fears, or someone has told you that something would be and you accepted it as a truth. Everything that happens, happens as an intentional act that is ordained through thought and emotion. Everything... You have accepted into your life precisely all that you have desired to accept, and you have experienced life according to your accepted values. It is you who determine what is good for you, what is to be accepted by you, what is to be experienced by you. It is you, by your own thinking. (Ramtha, *WB*, chapter 5)

I am primarily a personality with a message: you create the world that you know. You have been given perhaps the most awesome gift of all: the ability to project your thoughts outward into physical form. (Seth, *SS*, chapter 1)

Consider your present self as an actor in a play... You create the props, the settings, the themes; in fact you write, produce, and act in the entire production – you and every other individual who takes part. You are so focused in your roles, however, so intrigued by the reality that you have created, so entranced by the problems, challenges, hopes, and sorrows of your particular roles, that you have forgotten they are of your own creation. (Seth, *SS*, chapter 4)

I want you to realize that the responsibility for your life and your environment is your own. If you believe otherwise, then you are limited... As long as you believe your environment to be objective and independent of yourself, then to a large extent you feel powerless to change it, to see beyond it, or to imagine other alternatives that may be less apparent... In each life you choose and create your own settings or environments; and in this one you chose your parents and whatever childhood incidents that came within your experience. You wrote the script. Like a true absent-minded professor, the conscious self forgets all this, however, so when tragedy appears in the script, difficulty or challenges, the conscious self looks for someone or something to blame. (Seth, *SS*, chapter 4)

If you find yourself assailed by physical difficulties, however, you begin to wonder what is wrong. Sometimes you blame others, your own background, or a previous life – if you accept reincarnation. You may hold God or the devil responsible, or you may simply say, 'That is life,' and accept the negative experience as a necessary portion of your lot. You may finally come to a half-understanding of the nature of reality and wail, 'I believe that I have caused these ill effects, but I find myself unable to reverse them.' If this is the case, then regardless of what you have told yourself thus far, you still do not believe that you are the creator of your own experience. As soon as you recognize this fact you can begin at once to alter those conditions that cause you dismay or dissatisfaction. (Seth, *NPR*, Preface)

The most rejuvenating idea of all, and the greatest step to any true illumination, is the realization that your exterior life stems from the invisible world of your reality through your conscious thoughts and beliefs, for then you realize the power of your individuality and identity. You are immediately presented with choices. You can no longer see yourself as a victim of circumstances. (Seth, *NPR*, chapter 10)

There are no victims in this world... Neither are you a victim of the choices of others. At some level you have *all* created that which you say you detest – and, having created it, you have *chosen* it. This is an advanced level of thinking, and it is one which all Masters reach sooner or later. For it is only when they can accept responsibility for *all* of it that they can achieve the power to change *part* of it. So long as you entertain the notion that there is something or someone else out there 'doing it' to you, you disempower yourself to do anything about it. Only when you say 'I *did* this' can you find the power to change it. *It is much easier to change what you are doing than to change what another is doing.* (Walsch, *CWG I*, chapter 1)

The man who keeps marrying the same kind of woman – one who is all wrong for him – packaged in different forms, does not 'want' (desire, seek, consciously choose) to keep creating bad marriages. The person who hits a thumb with a hammer could not be said to have 'wanted' the experience. It was not desired, sought, consciously chosen. Yet all objective phenomena is drawn to you subconsciously; all events are created by you unconsciously; every person, place, or thing in your life was drawn to you by you – was self-created, if you will – to provide you with the exact and perfect conditions, the perfect opportunity, to experience what you next wish to experience as you go about the business of evolving. Nothing can happen – I say to you, nothing can occur – in your life which is not a precisely perfect opportunity for you to heal something, create something, or experience something that you wish to heal, create, or experience in order to be who you really are. (Walsch, *CWG III*, chapter 1)

time isn't continuous, so the 'past'
has no bearing on the present...

unless you let it

In this chapter we'll continue to examine some of the more startling implications that arise from our new model of supersoul consciousness, and confirm our responsibility for creating our reality *in the now*.

We'll begin with the concept of time and, although this is by no means intended as a scientific treatise on the subject, our sources are adamant that there's really no such thing as the 'past' or the 'future', there's only now. That doesn't mean I won't be continuing to use these words in the rest of the book, because it's almost impossible not to, and I won't be using quotes around them all the time because this would become tedious. But the point has been made.

To expand on this using ideas more fully explored in *Supersoul*, our perception of time as a continuous flow moving *from* the past, *through* the present and *into* the future is merely something we humans have developed to allow us to make sense of the physical world. Apart from anything else, with so much information flooding our senses and so great a desire to analyse it all, the ability to file away past events is what stops us from simply frying our brains.

But this perception of continuous flow is only that, a perception. As hard as it can be for most of us to understand, it might be more accurate to suggest that what we perceive as time is made up of 'a series of discrete snapshots of an eternal now that encompasses everything that we perceive as the past and future, but is nevertheless forever changing from now-moment to now-moment'.

key quotes

You cannot disconnect your past, present and future, for they are all one. (Abraham, *LOA*, part 4)

There is no such thing as past and future, there is only *now*. (Jeshua, *WOH*, lesson 3)

Time is a creation of the mind. Without the mind, time does not exist. In your dimension time, space, and movement are three separate elements of reality. When humanity reaches a higher degree of consciousness and with it an extended dimension, time, space, and movement begin to integrate more and more, until they become one. However, it is an error to believe that the next higher dimension is timelessness. There are many extended 'times', if I may use this expression, in the higher realms of being, long before you reach the state of being that is timeless... Time is a very limiting existential modality. It is a fragment, cut from a wider and freer dimension of experience. The limited fragment, called time, is at the disposal of human beings so that they can grow, fulfill themselves, experience, and reach happiness and liberation up to the limit commensurate with this dimension. (Pathwork, 1 Mar 63)

The past was simply a Now moment that was experienced and is no more... There is only the Isness of this Now. What is important is now. You are the product of Now. Your life is lived in the Now. Your future is created in the Now. (Ramtha, *WB*, chapter 13)

There is no time but *this* time. There is no moment but this moment. 'Now' is all there is. Everything that ever happened, is happening, and ever will happen, is happening right *now*... 'Time' is not a continuum. It is an element of relativity that exists vertically, not horizontally. Don't think of it as a 'left-to-right' thing – a so-called time line that runs from birth to death for each individual, and *from* some finite point *to* some finite point for the universe. 'Time' is an up-and-down thing! Think of it as a spindle, representing the eternal moment of now. Now picture leafs of paper on the spindle, one atop the other. These are the elements of time. Each element separate and distinct, yet each existing *simultaneously with all the others*. All the paper on the spindle at once! (Walsch, *CWG II*, chapter 3)

The eternal moment of now is forever changing. (Walsch, *CWG II*, chapter 19)

BE FULLY PRESENT IN EACH MOMENT OF NOW

Several of our sources were stressing this idea way before the success of Eckhart Tolle's seminal *The Power of Now* – to which this book's title owes much – but he brought it to an even greater audience. The reason it's hugely important to our theme is precisely because our sources stress that we creating our own reality in *each moment of now*.

The problem, as Tolle pointed out, is we spend the vast majority of our waking hours not enjoying the moment at all, but looking backwards or forwards – and in doing so we often insist on focusing on the more unpleasant aspects of our experience. So if we're dwelling on a past problem we're allowing unfavourable thoughts to influence our reality *now* – when what we should be doing is learning from it if necessary, then letting it go and just enjoying the now. Or if we're worrying about a possible future event we're again allowing unfavourable thoughts to influence our reality *now* – when what we should be doing is appreciating it's not a certainty, taking any actions we can now to produce a favourable outcome, then letting it go and just enjoying the now.

Either way by choosing to put our focus into something we regard as unfavourable we're giving it power in the now, and one way or another and to a greater or lesser extent it will influence our future now-moments. The trick, then, is to focus as much as possible on the present moment, and on extracting the maximum value or joy from it. Occasionally of course it will be appropriate to think about the apparent past or future, but when we do we should as much as possible focus on enjoyable thoughts and events rather on unpleasant or depressing ones.

key quotes

Your *now* is powerful. In fact, all of your power is right here, right now. (Abraham, *LOA*, part 5)

In each and every moment you are, literally, using that ceaseless and unlimited power to create. And you remain perfectly free at any time to create anew. What you will experience in your tomorrows is only the effect of which pebbles you are choosing to drop into the field of your awareness as thoughts *now*. (Jeshua, *WOH*, lesson 8)

People strive toward the future mainly for two reasons: you do not like the present and hope for something better from the future; or else you fear a certain aspect of life and want to leave it behind... Your vague hopes for the future and the unpleasant, unfulfilled state of the present are your reasons for straining away from the present and into the future. Thereby you avoid living in the now. If, however, you were to explore within yourself the reasons for your unfulfillment and the difficulties which cause you to strain away from them, you would be capable of living in the *now* fully, meaningfully, and dynamically, deriving all the many joys from each moment that you now overlook. (Pathwork, 1 Mar 63)

In the ongoingness of this Now, each moment is brand new... It is not the captive of yesterday... You are free to do anything you wish to do in this moment. That is the Father's love for you: the freedom and the power that he has given you to create each moment anew. No one is ruled by the past. Whatsoever you did a moment ago or a millennium ago, you do not have to pay for anytime... To truly live as an Isness in this Now is to live without laws and rules and regulations that inhibit the expression and expansion of self. When you live as an Isness, the only thing that ever matters is now – not the past, not the future, but now – for that is precisely where God lives. (Ramtha, *WB*, chapter 13)

You form your reality now... The present is your point of power. (Seth, *NPR*, chapter 15)

ALL LIVES ACROSS ALL HUMAN ERAS ARE HAPPENING SIMULTANEOUSLY

Our sources are pretty much united in confirming the point made in the Preface that the lives of the soul probes projected by the supersoul are happening alongside each other, *irrespective of what era they're operating in*. Again it's extremely hard to make logical sense of this with our human brains, but the consistency of our sources makes it impossible to conclude anything other than that the whole ensemble of lives in which we and all our fellow soul probes are engaged is an ongoing, dynamic and interactive process.

Lip service is regularly paid to this idea of simultaneous lives in spiritual literature of all kinds, but rarely are its implications properly brought out. What it means is there are no completed 'past lives' whose 'karma' feeds inexorably into our own – an idea we'll return to in the next section. What there is, instead, is an ongoing interaction between what I refer to as 'resonant souls', an idea first introduced in *Supersoul*. These effectively replace past-life personalities in our new model, and they are most likely those fellow souls from our supersoul with whom we strongly share personality traits or life challenges. I'd suggest these are the consciousnesses we're most likely to make contact with during 'past-life' regression.

The extent to which we actually interact with these resonant souls will vary, dependent not only on the degree of resonance we have with any of them, but also more generally on how open and receptive we are to their influence, and vice versa. Different people will have different approaches as to the extent to which ties with resonant souls should be fostered. Some who're particularly open may gain great insights from some of them during meditation and so on, which is obviously all to the good. Less receptive people will merely experience strong intuitions sometimes, and it'll usually be advantageous to be open to these even if their source is unclear. Nor should we lose sight of the favourable impact *we* can have on *them* by rising to and overcoming our own challenges.

On the other hand any of us can sometimes find ourselves experiencing strong, unhelpful emotions that may make *some* sense in terms of our own life, but can't be fully explained and seem to be somehow exacerbated. These could at least in part stem from the impact of resonant souls facing similar challenges but perhaps in a more intense form. In such cases we'd do well to make a conscious decision to block them. In more extreme cases a sensitive person may be able to resolve such issues by making contact with said souls and even attempting some degree of healing. For others some therapeutic assistance to uncover their source may be appropriate, but arguably more as a last than a first resort. We'll return to this issue in a later chapter.

The golden rule laid down by our sources seems to be that each of us is fundamentally responsible for creating our own experience in each moment of now, which means the ongoing experiences of other souls – however resonant – are fundamentally their own responsibility, not ours. Nor can they exert a strongly disruptive influence over us unless we believe they can and choose to let them.

key quotes

You do not think to yourselves of the influences that are pressing to you continuously. You hold many focuses [life personalities] within essence [supersoul]. You hold many alternates [probable selves] within one focus. Your future self, as you think of it, is also quite influencing of your present. This is not to say, once again, that you hold no objective control and direction, for you hold all. (Elias, 9 Feb 97)

You choose your focuses and project from essence simultaneously. Therefore, all of your focuses are being accomplished within the now. It is only within your perception that they appear to be past or future. (Elias, 28 Jun 97)

I do express often to individuals within this forum that all of your focuses are continuously influencing of each other and of this focus, as you also are continuously influencing of all of your other focuses. But your attention is in *this* focus, and your creations in this focus are *your* creations. They are purposeful, they are intentional, and they are the responsibility of this particular focus. Therefore, as you continue to direct your attention to this particular focus in which you hold your attention, you also empower yourselves much more and create much more of your own expression of freedom and your ability to manipulate energy intentionally within this focus. It offers you the opportunity to view *how* you create your reality, and that you *do* create your reality individually, that your choices are your choices. You hold free will. You are not subject or victim to *any* expression of energy within *any* area of consciousness. (Elias, 5 Nov 99)

It is not correct, therefore, to suppose that your actions in this life are caused by a previous existence, or that you are being punished in this life for crimes in a past one. The lives are simultaneous... There is instant communication and an instant, if you prefer, feedback system... One life is not buried in the past, disconnected from the present self and any future self as well. (Seth, *SS*, chapter 4)

When you think of reincarnation, you suppose a series of progressions. Instead the various lives grow out of what your inner self is. They are not thrust upon you by some outside agency. They are a material development, as your consciousness opens up and expresses itself in as many ways as possible. (Seth, *SS*, chapter 4)

What you understand of reincarnation, and of the time terms involved, is a very simplified tale indeed... Reincarnation, in its own way, is also a parable. It seems very difficult for you to understand that you live in many realities – and many centuries – at one time. (Seth, *SS*, chapter 22)

There is interaction between you and your reincarnational selves constantly... Those selves are not dead, in other words... Actions that you make now can help a so-called past personality; and a so-called future personality may step in and help you along your weary way. (Seth, *SS*, Appendix)

Reincarnation, as it is usually explained, in terms of one life before another, is a myth; but a myth enabling many to partially understand facts that they would otherwise dismiss – insisting as they do upon the concept of a continuity of time. (Seth, *SS*, Appendix)

[Your other] lives exist simultaneously. They are other expressions of yourself, interacting, but with each conscious self possessing the point of power in its own present. (Seth, *NPR*, chapter 15)

Since all is simultaneous, your present beliefs can alter your past ones, whether from this life or a 'previous' one. Existences are open-ended... *The point of power is in the present*. This experienced present also represents your psychic touchstone to all of your other existences... All of your other 'reincarnational selves'... are unconsciously aware of your conscious experience, as you are unconsciously aware of theirs. The interaction is constant, however, and in *all* of your presents, creative. You draw on their knowledge as they draw on yours, and this of course applies to personalities that you would *consider* future. You have a gigantic pool of information and experience to draw upon, but this will be utilized according to your present conscious beliefs. (Seth, *NPR*, chapter 19)

Within any given twenty-four hour period, then, traces and aspects of all your other experiences appear in their own way. You each contain aspects of your other identities within your current selves – some very obvious perhaps and others barely noticeable... The adventures of your simultaneous selves, again, appear as traces in your own consciousness, as ideas or daydreams or disconnected images, or sometimes even in sudden intuitions. They can be drawn upon, drawn out, to help you understand current problems. This does not mean that you will necessarily have a flood of reincarnational information, instant intuitive recognition of 'past' lives, or experience any such *intrusive* data. It does mean that in your own life such information automatically appears in intimate ways, but couched within the framework of your own comprehensions, even passing unobtrusively through your conscious thoughts... Impulses to try activities you have not tried before may indeed be messages from other portions of your own being. (Seth, *NPR*, chapter 19)

You are living *this* life, your presently realized life, in your past, your present, your future, all at once!.. You are also living other lives – what you call 'past lives' – right now as well, although you experience them as having been in your 'past' (if you experience them at all), and that is just as well. It would be very difficult for you to play this wonderful game of life if you had *full awareness* of what is going on.' (Walsch, *CWG II*, chapter 5)

Past, present, and future are concepts you have constructed, realities you have invented, in order to create a context within which to frame your present experience. Otherwise all of your experiences would be overlapping. They actually are overlapping – that is, happening at the same 'time' – you simply don't know this. You've placed yourself in a perception shell that blocks out the total reality. (Walsch, *CWG III*, chapter 2)

No individual aspect of divinity has power over any other aspect of divinity. It is not possible for one soul to affect another against its will. (Walsch, *CWG III*, chapter 14)

YOU CAN CREATE YOURSELF AFRESH BECAUSE PAST EXPERIENCES DON'T HAVE TO SHAPE NOW

We've seen that what might seem to be past lives can't affect us in any fixed way, partly because they're still going on, and partly because we also have ultimate control over whether we let any resonant souls influence us or not. But the perhaps even more important revelation is that what's happened in our apparent past *in this life* doesn't have to influence our experience of now either. Our point of power is *now*, not in the apparent past.

We saw in the Preface that our brains are naturally wired to use past associations to understand and react to our present. So how can our sources be all but unanimous that this is simply *not* how it *has* to be? The answer is that we can learn to rewire ourselves so we no longer operate using those past associations that don't serve us. An association such as 'hand in fire = burn = pain' remains a constructive one in most circumstances, whereas 'falling in love = rejection = pain', or 'new job = failure = dismissal', clearly aren't. At least theoretically, if our ability to discipline our thoughts meant we could divest ourselves of all unhelpful past associations, we could literally start with a clean sheet in each or any new moment of now, thereby creating an entirely different experience for ourselves.

The idea that for a true master the sky really is the limit will be confirmed in the final chapter, but any of us can put this theory into practice at least to some extent. For example, not long after I became fully aware of just how much power we have to reinvent ourselves, in the early stages of writing this book, I was faced with a situation in which an intense fear of lack of money reared its head due to a particular situation that triggered all sorts of past associations. Initially it was *so* intense it created a physical pain in my chest. But because these ideas were fresh in my mind I took control and insisted to myself that my *now* didn't *have* to be linked to, associated with or influenced by these past experiences. What's more I remained absolutely firm every time the fear tried to raise its ugly head. Within twenty-four hours a situation arose that unequivocally proved the link had been broken. I'm no master yet. If I can do this, any of us can – and on a far grander scale if we really put our minds to it.

We've also seen that our new model – based on simultaneous lives, and on complete free will to direct our adult experience for better or worse – means there can be no such thing as 'karmic law' whereby the past can irrevocably limit our choices in the present. Unless, of course, we choose to believe there is, in which case any form of such a law we decide to put our faith in will work perfectly.

But our sources are quite clear that this is really nonsense that turns us into victims, and denies us our true power to be whatever we want to be – and to change that whenever we feel like it.

More generally, if anyone wants to drag their past around with them like a ball and chain, and regale all and sundry with their woes, and why the situation they're in isn't their fault but that of their parents or siblings or ex-wife or business partner and so on and so forth – that's fine, it's entirely their *choice*. As we saw at the end of the last chapter nearly all us are attracted to playing the victim at some point in our lives, to a greater or lesser extent. But let's not fool ourselves into sympathy for such a limiting and disempowering view of life. Better to try to help the person take responsibility.

Of course at the same time as appreciating all this we should recognise that our past *decisions* do influence our present circumstances and environment. Indeed they determine where we live and how, with whom, what family and friends we have, our job and hobbies, how much money we have, and so on. But our past *beliefs* don't have to influence where we go from here. What's more, as a complete master, we could go from pauper to prince overnight – although I suspect most of us will be content to aim just a little lower.

I should point out here too that, if we find ourselves in a deep rut for any length of time – especially if it's in multiple areas of our life – then it can be much harder to sever the past associations and 'turn the juggernaut around'. This is an issue we'll return to in a later chapter.

key quotes

The details of any past physical experience do not affect you in this physical experience. There is much confusion about that, and it comes largely because there are those who do not want to accept that they are the creator of their own experience... *There is nothing from past-life experience that is influencing that which you are doing now, unless, in some way, you have become aware of it and are now giving it your attention.* (Abraham, *LOA*, part 3)

When you make any change, if you understand you are really, really, really, really, really, not the same person... it means that you really, in the next moment, are not the same person that was there a moment ago, and that the you you are now doesn't have the same history. You have no more connection to... the person that was there a moment ago, that you used to think you were. You are literally, at that moment, zero, free to be whatever you define, all the way up and down the timeline, because past and future come from the present, what you define in the present is what you are on all levels of experience, you change everything. (Bashar, *Fundamentals*)

You create your own reality! You choose your own choices for your own experiences, within each moment of physical existence. Therefore, you are not the victim of your past experiences... In this, you engage another belief system, that you have been taught and influenced, throughout your focus, by other individuals who have exercised control over you. (Elias, 30 Jun 96)

We are presently battling very established belief systems. Whether you acknowledge within yourselves these belief systems or not, they exist. You also hold a belief system in karma. Whether you understand this term or whether you have studied this concept or not, you hold the belief system. It is a mass belief system. You believe that if you are experiencing any element that is harmful to another, this shall be to your detriment and you shall owe for this. Therefore, you shall manifest to be making payment. This is not true. It is a belief system. It reinforces your ideas of right and wrong and good and bad. It reinforces your belief systems of illness or oddities, but these are all choices. You all choose. No thing is thrust upon you. As I have stated, you may not instantaneously objectively understand your creations; but as we speak, you learn to learn your own language once again, and therefore you begin to understand your creation of your own manifestations, and the why's. (Elias, 2 Feb 97)

I, alone, am the literal creator of my moment-to-moment experience. (Jeshua, *WOH*, lesson 8)

At any moment as you go along in your experience, as you experience the reverberation, the coming back of the ripples you have sent out, in that very moment you are not a victim of what you have created... You are free to choose how you will experience the effect of that ripple. And if you experience it with unconditional freedom, with unconditional acceptance and love, forgiveness, neutrality and innocence, you literally defuse the effects of that ripple upon the pool of your consciousness. And then, in that moment, you become instantly free to begin creating, in a new way, the ripples that you will experience in the future. And that is why you are never a victim of anyone's creation, especially your own... We are seeking to share with you how infinitely *free* you are. There are many in your world that teach this illusory doctrine of what is called karma – that what you send out now you *must* experience sooner or later, and how you experience it is directly related to the quality of the ripple you sent out. *That is not true*. That would make you a victim. (Jeshua, *WOH*, lesson 9)

What you term karma is not the law of God; it is the law of those who believe in it. Unfortunately, there are multitudes who believe in this doctrine... They believe that whatever they do in life, they must come back and pay for in the next one. Everything that happens to them they continuously attribute to karmic fulfillment. But that is a very poor explanation for life. It deserves much more than that... The true lawgiver is each sovereign entity, for each possesses an ego that accepts truth. And whatever he calls truth, whatever he creates as a law in his being, so it will be... If you choose to believe in karma, you will certainly be at the hands of your own creation, for you have given power to that belief. (Ramtha, *WB*, chapter 13)

You usually do not realize that your physical body is created by you at each moment as a direct result of your inner conception of what you are, or that it changes in important chemical and electromagnetic ways with the ever-moving pace of your own thought... You are constantly changing the form, the shape, the contour, and the meaning of your physical body and most intimate environment, although you do your best to ignore these constant alterations. (Seth, *SS*, chapter 2)

Many schools of thought over-emphasize the effects of reincarnational existences, so that often they explain present-life circumstances as a result of rigid and uncompromising patterns determined in a 'past' life. You will feel relatively incompetent to handle present physical reality, to alter your environment, to affect and change your world, if you feel that you are at the mercy of conditions over which you have no control. The reasons given for such subjugations matter little in the long run, for the reasons change with the times and with your culture. You are not under a sentence placed upon you for original sin, by any childhood events, or by past-life experience. (Seth, *SS*, chapter 4)

You cannot justify or rationalize present circumstances by saying, 'This is because of something I did in a past life,' for within yourself now is the ability to change negative influences. (Seth, *SS*, chapter 12)

It is important that you realize that spiritual ignorance is at the basis of so many of your problems, and that indeed your only limitations are spiritual ones. (Seth, *SS*, chapter 21)

You are not, therefore, at the mercy of any neurosis from a past life, nor are there any fears from your present lives that you cannot conquer... You cannot be threatened in this life by fears from your early childhood, or by so-called past existences, unless you so thoroughly believe in the nature of fear that you allow yourselves to be conquered by it. Each of your personalities are free to accept and develop, from the miraculous banks of reality, those experiences and emotions that you want, and to reject those you do not want. (Seth, *SS*, Appendix)

If you accept the idea that the reasons for your behavior are forever buried in the past of this life, or any other, then you will not be able to alter your experience until you change that belief. (Seth, *NPR*, chapter 2)

There is no karma to be paid off as punishment unless you *believe* that there are crimes for which you must pay. In larger terms there is no cause and effect either, though these are root assumptions in your reality. (Seth, *NPR*, chapter 9)

Those of you who believe in reincarnation in more or less conventional terms, can make the error of using or blaming 'past' lives, organizing them through your current beliefs. It is bad enough to believe that you are at the mercy of *one* past, but to consider yourself helpless before innumerable previous errors from other lives puts you in an impossible situation; the conscious will is robbed of its power to act. (Seth, *NPR*, chapter 15)

There is no such thing as karmic debt... A debt is something that must or should be repaid. *You are not obligated to do anything.* Still, there are certain things that you *want* to do; choose to experience. And some of these choices hinge on – the desire for them has been created by – what you have experienced before... If karma is the innate desire to do better, to be bigger, to evolve and to grow, and to look at past events and experiences as a measure of that, then, yes, karma does exist. *But it does not require anything*. Nothing is ever required. You are, as always you have ever been, a being of free choice. (Walsch, *CWG I*, chapter 14)

You are creating yourself anew in each moment of now. (Walsch, *CWG II*, chapter 12)

physical reality is nothing
more than a mirror...

it only reflects what
you put out

Having dispensed with the more obvious objections to the idea that we're entirely responsible for creating our own reality, and also some of the more limiting *spiritual* beliefs around the subject, let's turn our attention to the real underlying workings of the law of attraction.

Our sources are again united in the view that the reality we experience can be thought of as an encircling mirror that reflects back to us the contents of our minds and hearts. Sometimes this is very obvious because there's hardly any time lag between the thought or act and its reflection back to us. But more often, while our thoughts remain largely uncontrolled and often contradictory as they meander through hundreds of topics every day, there's a delay in the reflection. This makes it much harder to recognise that *everything* around us is, nevertheless, an accurate but dynamic and multidimensional reflection of all our strongest and most-prevalent thoughts and beliefs from previous now-moments.

key quotes

To better understand the Law of Attraction, see yourself as a magnet attracting unto you the essence of that which you are thinking and feeling. (Abraham, *LOA*, part 2)

Physiological reality, take me literally, is a mirror, it is just a more complex mirror, a holographic mirror, a multidimensional mirror, so that you don't always recognize all the reflections as you. But believe me, they are, all the reflections are you, and I mean literally every object, person, place and thing, every situation, every circumstance, every moment of time and space is you being reflected back to yourself, from the particular point of view you chose to express at that particular moment... The idea to understand, therefore, is that if you want to see a smile reflected in that mirror you have to smile first, or there will be no reflection of a smile. (Bashar, *Fundamentals*)

Every action in every moment within your reality, you are

projecting energy. There is not one moment within your reality that you are not outputting energy, and that energy that you are outputting precisely draws to you the same. You automatically draw the same energy that you project. You can all visualize in this moment. Close your eyes. Visualize your body, standing. Extending from your body is a shockwave of energy that is moving outward in the thrust, the intensity and the distance of a nuclear explosion in this moment. That is how powerful your energy is. The power of that energy, as it creates that shockwave that extends outwardly, generates an action as a magnet, the most powerful magnet that you can imagine. That magnet will pull to it any expression that matches what you are projecting. It will intentionally seek out any expression, any manifestation that matches the energy that is being expressed. (Elias, 17 Mar 07)

The formula for creating is very simple... you project energy, you reflect energy, and you either react to the reflection or you choose in relation to the reflection... Every moment you are projecting energy. Knowing or being aware of what type of energy you are projecting in any moment is not as easy for it is very unfamiliar to you. It is not hidden from you, for you have created this marvelous design in your reality in which every moment that you project you are reflecting. Therefore, the reflection of what you are doing is always in front of you. How you pay attention to that reflection is questionable. What you do with that reflection is the tricky aspect, for what you generally do with most reflections is react to them! (Elias, 22 Oct 11)

The first step in awakening is to allow into the mind this axiom of truth: Nothing that you experience is caused by anything outside of you. You experience only the effects of your own choices. (Jeshua, *WOH*, lesson 1)

As you have attracted to yourselves certain persons, places, things, objects and, above all, thoughts, beliefs and perceptions, you have dropped them like little pebbles into the still clear pool of your vast and eternal awareness. What you experience are the effects, or the ripples, of those pebbles. They literally join with other ripples that you have created. As these ripples move out and touch one another and come back to you, this is the field of creation that makes up your physical, third-dimension reality. (Jeshua, *WOH*, lesson 8)

The world around you will over a period of time coagulate, create itself in a context that will *mirror* to you that which seems to prove the negative thought by now you have forgotten you even created. Then you will have the negative thought again and you will mistakenly believe that the negative thought is there *because of* the conditions outside of you. (Jeshua, *WOK*, lesson 5)

You do not know that you have molded what you experience in this moment in such a precise way that there can be no mistake concerning it. As I have often said, the sum total of all your conscious, semi-conscious, unconscious, explicit and implicit thoughts, beliefs, assumptions, intentions, feelings, emotions and will directions – conflicting as they may be – creates your present experience and the way your life unfolds for you. Your present life expresses your inner state exactly, like a faultless mathematical equation. Thus you can use your life as a map into your inner regions. (Pathwork, 9 Feb 73)

How is your future created? Through thought. All of your tomorrows are designed by your thoughts this very day, for every thought you entertain – every fantasy you have, for whatever emotional purpose – creates a feeling within your body which is recorded within your soul. That feeling then sets a precedent for the conditions in your life, for it will draw to you circumstances that will create and match the same feeling that has been recorded in your soul. And know that every word you utter is creating your days to come, for words are only sounds that express the feelings within your soul that have been given birth through thought. (Ramtha, *WB*, chapter 5)

First of all, you must understand that no objective reality exists but that which is created by consciousness. Consciousness always creates form, and not the other way around... Your own physical reality is created in perfect replica of your inner desires and thoughts. (Seth, *SS*, chapter 2)

You are used to the idea that you express yourselves directly through words... Physical objects are the result of another kind of expression. You create them as surely as you create words. (Seth, *SS*, chapter 5)

There are no real divisions between the perceiver and the thing seemingly perceived. In many ways the thing perceived is an extension of the perceiver. (Seth, *SS*, chapter 6)

The universe is just a big Xerox machine. It simply produces multiple copies of your thoughts. (Walsch, *CWG I*, chapter 11)

THE EVIDENCE OF THE ASTRAL

The idea that our reality only mirrors our thoughts is backed up by the broader context of the immediate 'thought responsiveness' of other planes of consciousness – particularly the 'astral' planes. This is a topic I explore in far more detail in volume two of this series, *Afterlife*, but for now suffice to say that the views of several of our sources are confirmed by other channelled material and, even more, by modern out-of-body pioneers.

key quotes

Your physical world, earth, is a nice environment for fine-tuning your knowledge, for here your thoughts do not translate into an instant equivalent – you have a 'buffer of time'... If you were in a dimension where you were instantly manifesting, you would be spending more of your time trying to get rid of your mistakes (as many of you are doing now anyway) than you would in creating the things you want. (Abraham, *LOA*, part 3)

When you adopt a human body and the ego state in this three-dimensional world, you automatically close off the memory of other states of consciousness. These forgotten states are much less confined, much freer, much more aware. In them you were completely capable of molding your life, to a degree that the human consciousness cannot possibly comprehend. (Pathwork, 9 Feb 73)

In the physical life there might be a lapse between thought and experience. In the spirit realms there is no lapse; results are instantaneous. Newly departed souls therefore learn to monitor their thoughts very carefully, because whatever they think of, they experience. (Walsch, *CWG III*, chapter 3)

MANY LIMITING BELIEFS ARE CULTURALLY IMPRESSED

We now turn our attention to the issue of limiting beliefs – those that literally *restrict* our ability to create joy and abundance in our lives. We'll start with the many, many beliefs that are culturally impressed upon us, increasingly so in the modern world of mass communication and the internet. They all tend to be based on fear.

In the Western world at least, politicians have a vested interest in making us fear burglars, or vandals, or terrorists, or immigrants – to unite us under their banner as the only people who can save us, to make us subservient and obedient, and to divert our attention from the more dubious aspects of their own behaviour. A huge insurance industry is founded on the principle of fear of loss and of ill-health, and in some cases is ensconced in law. For all that many individual health professionals do a wonderful, underpaid job in extremely trying conditions, pharmaceutical giants and the medical profession generally have a vested interest in inventing as many new illnesses as they can, and the drugs to cure them. Some people are constantly glued to the internet researching any new ailment whose symptoms they can spot and then exacerbate in themselves. Old people are encouraged to expect decrepitude and ill-health. Huge advertising campaigns run by well-meaning health charities do everything they can to keep *their* disease or illness at the forefront of people's minds. We're all encouraged to go for a bewildering array of health checks at regular intervals.

How many of us ever stop to question all this? How many of us recognise that we can *choose* not to attract *any* of this into our lives – simply by divesting ourselves of the limiting beliefs, and by concentrating on more desirable outcomes instead. In terms of health and diet, many people have now learned not to listen to the constant stream of conflicting 'expert' advice from university research teams sponsored to come up with a finding of some sort about different food stuffs. Instead they use their own inner guidance and common sense about what's right for their body and what isn't. By concentrating on our psychological approach to food, Seth even turns conventional notions of healthy eating and of dieting on their heads.

On a slightly broader tack, he and Jeshua suggest we should question *all* the 'values' we've built up over the years. So you might want to try some other experiments too. For example, stop locking your car, or your house. Just surround them with a bubble of white light and *know* that this attitude will mean those who might want to steal simply *won't* be attracted into *your* reality.

Seth also suggests we should question the stereotypical 'roles' we place ourselves in, like 'mother' or 'breadwinner', while Jeshua goes further and encourages us to understand that we don't *need* to do or think *anything at all* that we don't want to.

key quotes

The steady offering of details of illness is very influential in the increasing of sickness in your society. If you allow yourself to focus on the constant barrage of unpleasant statistics regarding the never-ending stream of possible physical maladies, it cannot help but affect your personal *point of attraction*... The more you think about illness and worry about illness – the more you attract illness.

(Abraham, *LOA*, part 2)

As you hear the statistics of what percentage of your population will be robbed this year, you must understand that the numbers are so high and getting higher because so many people are being stimulated by the thought. Those *warnings* do not protect you from robberies, but instead make them more likely. They do such a good job of making you aware of the prevalence of robberies... that you not only think of it with emotion – but you expect it. (Abraham, *LOA*, part 2)

Notice, in your society, that the more that is offered regarding any topic, the greater the public *expectancy* of it. In the same way the greater the *expectancy* of the individuals, the greater the likelihood is that they will attract it. (Abraham, *LOA*, part 4)

You do not have to survive. Whoever told you that you *had* to? You do not have to make everybody happy. Whoever told you that you had to? Whoever told you that you *could* make anybody happy? You do not have to abide as a body in space and time. Whoever told you that you had to? You do not have to pay your bills. Who told you that? You literally *need* do nothing... For how can there be the power of freedom to choose and to create when you are being governed by the belief of the world that you must be a certain way? The belief that you need to be acceptable to others, that you need to conform and fit in, that you need to dress the way others dress, and that you need to be committed to surviving an extra day upon this plane? There can be no freedom where there is need. (Jeshua, *WOH*, lesson 2)

Where have you said, 'I will allow neutrality to all events in *this* sphere, but not in *that* sphere. If my friends divorce or separate, well okay, I'll see that as neutral. But if my spouse leaves me, that is not neutral... If the streams in a country on the other side of the world from where I am become polluted because the consciousness of a community allowed a factory to be built without safeguards, well, it's on the other side of the world, a neutral event. But if they build it in my backyard, it is no longer neutral.' It is always wise to look lovingly to see where you have drawn the line, to see what you will look upon as neutral and what you cling to as being filled with meaning and value that is unquestionable... When you place a value upon something and then become adamant that that value exists in the event or the object outside of you, you have secured your place in fear... Look to see where you are emotionally enmeshed with the value you have placed upon anything or anyone. Any relationship whatsoever. (Jeshua, *WOH*, lesson 9)

For example, [you might say] 'I can't eat that because that's a very bad substance, and I want to be healthy.' It is the very fear that is creating a tomorrow of unhealthiness. (Jeshua, *WOK*, lesson 4)

Somewhere it is the nature of your thought – the agreements you have made unconsciously or consciously about what things mean, the agreements you have made with the family and the culture in which you have been birthed – that has actually generated the energy that is showing up as the effects you experience as your life. (Jeshua, *WOK*, lesson 5)

Listen to your own conversation as you speak with friends, and to theirs. See how you reinforce each other's beliefs. See how your imaginations often follow the same lines. All of this is quite out in the open if you realize that it is. (Seth, *NPR*, chapter 4)

You will primarily organize your experience along definite lines. It may be your sex role or your professional role. You may see yourself as a mother or a father first of all, as a teacher, an editor, or as a 'man's man'. You will, however, emphasize one certain quality above all others – your athletic nature, your spiritual bent, whatever it may be. Now such concentration is excellent if the original concept continues to expand with your experience, and of itself is not limiting to a strong degree. You may see yourself primarily as a mother. Initially, that may simply involve taking care of your children at home. But if that idea of yourself remains limited then it may preclude, say, even being a wife to your husband, deny you many complementary interests, and prevent expansion of your personality in other areas. (Seth, *NPR*, chapter 11)

It is impossible to separate your daily experience in any of its aspects from your beliefs and those judgments that you place upon them. The beliefs boil down to your ideas of right and wrong, and they involve all of your attitudes concerning illness and health, wealth and poverty, the relationships of the races, religious conflicts, and more important, your intimate day-by-day psychological reality. (Seth, *NPR*, chapter 12)

You may be convinced that human nature is evil, or that no one is safe from another's aggression, or that people are motivated mainly by greed. Such beliefs attract their own reality. If you have anything worth losing, you are then automatically convinced that someone else will take it from you, or try their hardest to do so. In your own way you send out messages to just such a person... Each belief can be seen as a powerful [radio] station, pulling to it from fields of probabilities only those signals to which it is attuned, and blocking out all others. When you set up a new station there may be some static or bleed-through from the old one for a while. (Seth, *NPR*, chapter 15)

Your doctors impress upon each individual in your culture that you must have a physical examination every six months or you will get cancer; that you must have medical insurance because you will become ill... Modern physicians'... suggestions *bring about* diseases which are diagnosed *in advance*. You are told what to look for... You are paying in advance for illness that you are certain will come your way. You are making all preparations in the present for a future of illness. You are betting upon disease and not health... Even more unfortunate are the special policies for the elderly that detail in advance all of the most stereotyped and distorted concepts about health and age. There is a great correlation between the kind of policies that people take out, and the illnesses that they then fall prey to. (Seth, *NPR*, chapter 16)

You are what you *think*, not what you eat – and to a large extent what you *think about* what you eat is far more important. What you think about your body, health and illness will determine how your food is used, and how your chemistry handles fats, for instance, or carbohydrates. Your attitudes in preparing meals are highly important. Physically, it is true, but again generally speaking, that your body needs certain nourishments. But within that pattern there is great leeway, and the organism itself has the amazing capacity to make use of substitutes and alternatives... A belief in health can help you utilize a 'poor' diet to an amazing degree. [Whereas] the best diet in the world, by anyone's standards, will not keep you healthy if you have a belief in illness... If you are convinced that a specific food will give you a particular disease, it will indeed do so. (Seth, *NPR*, chapter 16)

Let us take another example, a very simple one. You are overweight. It is a physical fact. It grieves you, but you believe it completely. You begin a round of diets, all based on the idea that you are overweight *because* you eat too much. Instead, *you eat too much because you believe that you are overweight*. The physical picture always fits because your belief in being overweight conditions your body to behave in just such a manner... Momentary gains will not last. (Seth, *NPR*, chapter 16)

MOST ILLNESS ORIGINATES IN THE MIND, BUT CAN BE OVERCOME WITH KNOWING FAITH

Most of our sources, I suspect keen to make a point, are emphatic that *all* illness originates in the mind and is merely a physical reflection of accumulated thoughts, behaviours and beliefs. I have deliberately used the term 'most' in the heading to allow for the possible exception of new challenges accepted in adulthood as an expansive development rather than as a result of limiting beliefs and so on, as discussed in the first chapter. Nevertheless it would probably be wrong to assume these are anything other than rare exceptions to the general rule.

Our sources talk about the detrimental effect constant worry and, worse still, emotions like hatred can have on our physical bodies. But one issue particularly emphasised by Jeshua is the damage that being judgmental of others can do. Of course it'll come as no surprise that this isn't an ideal way to behave, but few of us probably stop to think how debilitating its effects *on us* are. What's more I suspect few of us notice just how much time we spend judging others, even if only mildly. Sometimes it can even appear to be something of a guilty pleasure, indulging in a bit of gossip or mickey-taking banter about someone else. But once we become sensitive to our true inner feelings the limiting energy of judgment will *never* feel good.

The other aspect mentioned by our sources in this section is that, just as the mind has the ability to create illness, it has equal ability to cure it. So as always 'knowing' faith in being cured can literally work wonders. What's more we all know of fine people who have proved this point and astounded doctors by, for example, overcoming supposedly terminal cancer – sometimes with no conventional medical intervention at all.

Although it's not directly relevant, I've also included a quote from Seth about our obsession with prolonging life at all costs, rather than letting nature take its course. Needless to say this is a direct result of us having lost the spiritual knowledge that death is not an ending but a new beginning.

key quotes

Every thought that you think that is directed *toward what you want* for your future is of great benefit to you. Every thought that you are thinking about your future that *you do not want* is a disadvantage to you. As you think of vitality and health – and want it and expect it in your future – you are prepaving and preparing that for yourself. But as you fear and worry about decline and disease, you are also prepaving or preparing *that* for your future. (Abraham, *LOA*, part 5)

Judgment causes the cellular structure to break down. If you could see this, you would never judge again. When you judge, even the cells in your body go crazy. They vibrate in a completely dissonant way. There is contraction. The fluids do not move through the cells. The nutrients do not become transported or delivered to the cells. The waste matter is not processed properly. Everything gets clogged up, and there is dis-ease. (Jeshua, *WOH*, lesson 3)

You are a conduit of energy... When you judge, it is as though you contracted and made the walls of the conduit smaller, just like building up rust in your pipes. And the flow becomes less and less. As you forgive judgments, it is as though the rust in the pipes is dissolving... Judgment is contraction. Forgiveness is relaxation, peace, trust and faith. (Jeshua, *WOH*, lesson 3)

If someone wrongs you and you spend your energy convincing them that they have wronged you, that you have a right to be angry and to be attacking in any way, you call to yourself – even into the cells of the body – the energy of conflict, judgment, war, death, disease, unhappiness and separation, *instantly!* (Jeshua, *WOH*, lesson 9)

Those portions of your brain that have not been activated at the present have the ability – simply through knowing – to reconstruct any damaged part within your body, wherever it is. The moment you know your body can heal itself, that thought sends a greater spark through the central nervous system to where the damaged part is, which will cause the DNA factor within each cell to clone and reconstruct the cell perfectly. Perfectly. You think that is miraculous? That is the way it should be and is... There are entities who have sought out healers, knowing that what they would hear would be an absolute truth. And by knowing it, it became an absolute truth within the embodiment; thus they were healed in a moment. That is what knowingness does, and it can change your body to however you want it to be. (Ramtha, *WB*, chapter 18)

Any physical ailment is symbolic of an inner reality or statement. Your entire life is a statement in physical terms. (Seth, *SS*, Appendix)

All healings are the result of the acceptance of one basic fact: that matter is formed by those inner qualities that give it vitality, that structure follows expectation, that matter at any time can be completely changed by the activation of the creative faculties inherent in all consciousness. (Seth, *NPR*, Preface)

If on the other hand you carry the idea too far – that illness can also be a learning process – then you can fall into the other extreme, glorifying sickness or disease as a necessary ennobling experience in which the body is purged so that the soul can be saved. Following such a belief, you will confuse suffering with saintliness, desolation with purity, and the denial of the body as spirituality and a badge of holiness. (Seth, *NPR*, chapter 12)

Illnesses usually represent unfaced problems, in your terms, and these dilemmas embody challenges meant to lead you to greater achievement and fulfillment. Because body and mind operate so well together, one will attempt to cure the other, and will often succeed if left alone. The organism has its own beliefs in health that are unconscious on your part. (Seth, *NPR*, chapter 17)

For all practical purposes the ill are put into prison [hospital]. They are forced to concentrate upon their condition... The individual is made to feel powerless, at the mercy of doctors or nurses who often do not have the time or energy to be personable, or to explain his or her condition in terms that can be understood. The patient is therefore forced to transfer his own sense of power to others, which further deepens his misery; this in turn reinforces the sense of powerlessness that initiated his condition. (Seth, *NPR*, chapter 17)

The medical profession often takes care to see that every

technological advance is brought to bear to force the self to remain within its flesh, when naturally soul and flesh would part. There are normal interlocking mechanisms that prepare the self for death, even chemical interactions that make this easier physically – burst of acceleration, in your terms, to propel the individual easily out of the body. Drugs can only hamper this. (Seth, *NPR*, chapter 17)

All illness is self-created... Worry is just about the worst form of mental activity there is – next to hate, which is deeply self destructive. Worry is pointless. It is wasted mental energy. It also creates biochemical reactions which harm the body, producing everything from indigestion to coronary arrest, and a multitude of things in between... Hatred is the most severely damaging mental condition. It poisons the body, and its effects are virtually irreversible... Worry, hate, fear – together with their offshoots: anxiety, bitterness, impatience, avarice, unkindness, judgmentalness, and condemnation – all attack the body at the cellular level. It is impossible to have a healthy body under these conditions... All illness is created in the mind first. (Walsch, *CWG I*, chapter 13)

Nothing occurs in your life – nothing – which is not first a thought. Thoughts are like magnets, drawing effects to you. The thought may not always be obvious, and thus clearly causative, as in, 'I'm going to contract a terrible disease'. The thought may be (and usually is) far more subtle than that. 'I am not worthy to live.' My life is always a mess.' 'I am a loser.' 'God is going to punish me.' 'I am sick and tired of my life!' Thoughts are very subtle, yet extremely powerful, forms of energy. Words are less subtle, more dense. Actions are the most dense of all... When you think, say *and* act out a negative concept such as 'I am a loser', you place tremendous creative energy into motion. Small wonder that you come down with a cold. That would be the least of it. (Walsch, *CWG I*, chapter 13)

It is very difficult to reverse the effects of negative thinking once they have taken physical form. Not impossible – but very difficult. It takes an act of extreme faith. It requires an extraordinary belief in the positive force of the universe... Healers have just such faith. It is a faith that crosses over into absolute knowing... It has the power to move mountains – to say nothing of molecules in your body. That is why healers can heal, often even at a distance. (Walsch, *CWG I*, chapter 13)

BECOME AWARE OF AND CONTROL YOUR LIMITING THOUGHTS

Given what we've just learned about the causes of physical illness, it's an unfortunate fact of life that as human beings, at least in the angst-ridden modern Western world, we tend to allow negative thoughts to proliferate – often inflaming a current situation by using past associations that may be completely irrelevant. These then breed more thoughts that repeat and repeat, and so on. Again there can almost be an attraction to wallowing in negativity sometimes, and undoubtedly it's related to the 'inner victim' we nearly all possess. But before we know it we can be in a real downward spiral. It's much better and easier to catch the thoughts early, and change them.

We'll see in future chapters that sometimes we need to spend some time evaluating a particularly persistent negative thought to find its source, and also that in cases of extreme anxiety or depression the advice to simply change the direction of our thoughts is easier said than done. But for most of us, most of the time, it's just about developing 'mindfulness'. That is, the ability of the objective 'observer self' that exists within all of us to flag up what's going on so we can deliberately change where we choose to place our focus – shifting it away from thoughts about things we don't want that make us unhappy, and onto things we do want that make us happy.

I indicated in the Preface that this book is at least as much about *not* reactively and unconsciously attracting those things we *don't* want as it is about proactively attracting those specific things we *do*, and cultivating this kind of mindfulness doesn't have to be connected to creating *specific outcomes* in our life. 'Things that make us happy' can be as simple as enjoying nature or our family or whatever – everyday things. Focusing on memories of things we've enjoyed, and thoughts about doing them more in the future, or about new things we think we might enjoy, are constructive and expansive. We don't *have* to be concentrating on being thinner or more attractive, or having more money and a better job, or attracting the perfect partner, and so on – although there's nothing intrinsically wrong with any of these. Yet for some people a general focus on attracting more love and joy into their life is far more constructive than trying to achieve more specific outcomes, and it may well prove easier too. We'll return to this in a later chapter.

key quotes

As you are focused upon a little negative thought, you will feel a little unwanted negative emotion. And if you are sensitive to the way you feel and want to feel better, you will change the thought. It is easy to change it when it is a small thought and a small emotion. It is much harder to change when it is a big thought and therefore a big emotion... The longer you stay focused upon what you do not want, the greater and more powerful that thought will become. But if you are sensitive to your emotions and you withdraw your attention from the unwanted subject very quickly, you will begin to feel better, and you will stop the attraction of this unwanted thing. (Abraham, *LOA*, part 2)

What we have noticed as we have been interacting with physical beings is that while you may have an experience that only lasts five or ten minutes, and while that experience may be unpleasant and uncomfortable, the majority of your negative emotion comes forth not *during* the minutes of that negative experience, but they come forth in all the hours that you ponder and chew upon it *after* the experience. Usually, there is much more of your time spent in thought of the negative thing that *has* happened than in the actuality of what *is* happening. (Abraham, *LOA*, part 5)

If an individual is agitated, or sad, or anxious, or angry, or frustrated, or irritated, or depressed, they continue to pay attention to that, and they perpetuate that feeling, for it is attractive, regardless that they do not like it, regardless that they label it as bad, regardless that it is uncomfortable, it is nonetheless attractive, and therefore, the individual continues to pay attention to it – very similar to physical feelings which are also signals. If an individual is experiencing pain, that physical feeling is attractive; it is designed to be attractive, that you will pay attention to it, but the point is that it is designed to be a signal, therefore, it is only necessary for you to pay attention to it to recognize that there is a message... To stop, look in a different direction... As your red light... But rather than recognizing it quickly as a signal, what you will generally do is you will pay attention to the feeling of being frustrated, and you will begin thinking about how frustrated you are. Now you are involving your thinking. Thinking, very easily, as we have discussed many, many times moves in the direction of repeat. (Elias, 15 Mar 13)

Awakening requires the act of vigilance and discipline. The discipline to cultivate a way of living in which you observe your own thoughts, in which you listen to the words that are coming out of your mouth, in which you observe the feelings that are evoked within your body. (Jeshua, *WOH*, lesson 3)

Your daily mind activity goes on and on, unobserved by your critical evaluation so that you are completely unaware of how your thought processes run in the same unproductive, negative channels. Nor do you perceive that you even derive a sort of satisfaction from allowing this to go on... The difficulty lies primarily in your not knowing, your not listening or giving attention to, your not observing what can be listened to, what can be observed once you look and listen into the right direction. When you observe the negative thinking processes, it is important to realize (a) what they do to you, how they connect with the very results you deplore most in your life, and (b) that you have the power to alter these thinking processes and find new channels, new ways of self-expression for your thinking. These two facets will make all the difference in the world... But first you must see yourself pursuing negative thought processes; see yourself brooding in the same vicious circles; see yourself almost willfully pursuing the same roundabout, very limited, very narrowly confined channels of thinking and never venturing beyond these fences, which are there to be taken by the leap of your own thinking. (Pathwork, 2 Sep 69)

To change your world you must change your thoughts. You must become consciously aware of what you tell yourself is true every moment of the day, for that is the reality that you project outward. (Seth, *SS*, Appendix)

You are not nearly as familiar with your own thoughts as you may imagine. They can escape from you like water through your fingers, carrying with them vital nutrients that spread across the landscape of your psyche – and all too often carrying sludge and mud that clog up the channels of experience and creativity. (Seth, *NPR*, Preface)

So much of your present experience is based on your previous thought. Thought leads to experience, which leads to thought, which leads to experience. This can produce constant joy when the sponsoring thought is joyous. It can, and does, produce continual hell when the sponsoring thought is hellatious. The trick is to change the sponsoring thought. (Walsch, *CWG I*, chapter 11)

YOU'RE ALWAYS CREATING MORE SOMETHING, AND ABUNDANCE IS JUST AS EASY AS LACK

I'm not sure if I'm typical, but one of the things that came as a revelation to me was our sources emphasising that creating *isn't* a choice. We're *always* doing it, in each moment of now. Unless our minds are completely blank – which is rare, except for experienced meditators – we're always thinking something and that will always be having some degree of impact on the future we're creating for ourselves. This has important implications. We might assume that if we're concentrating really hard on expansive outcomes or joyful thoughts for certain deliberately focused 'creative periods' each day – during meditation or whatever – then we can probably 'get away with' quite a lot of mild negativity the rest of the day. Not so! The message of our sources is that we need to be rather more vigilant than that.

Yet it's important not to go over the top about this, and as always balance is the key. As human beings even the greatest masters probably don't control every single thought they have in every single moment, and for most of us such a goal would instinctively feel like hard work – even as if it was taking all the joy and spontaneity out of life. So there are two riders to this warning that we're always creating. First, thoughts that are merely fleeting or have little emotion attached to them have little creative power. It's the repeated thoughts, especially ones that engender strong emotions, which have the most impact. Second, we'll see in later chapters that, rather than monitoring our every thought, simply paying attention to our emotional state – how we *feel* – will reliably tell us whether we're on the right track or not; and this is much easier.

The other aspect stressed by our sources, which may not be immediately obvious to all, is that creating abundance is *just as easy* as creating lack. So, given that we're creating all the time, we may as well be focusing on the former rather than the latter.

key quotes

You get the essence of what you are thinking about, whether it is something you want or something that you do not want. (Abraham, *LOA*, part 2)

You are *always* utilizing it [the Law of Attraction], whether you know that you are or not. You cannot stop utilizing it, for it is inherent in everything that you do. (Abraham, *LOA*, part 2)

Do not give thought to that which you do not want – for your attention to it attracts it... However, when you say, 'I'm not going to think about that subject any more,' in that moment you are still thinking about that subject. So the key is to think about something else – something that you *do* want. (Abraham, *LOA*, part 3)

You interact with other individuals, and you are all interconnected, and you each generate your own choices, and you do not create other individuals' realities, but you do create the image of every other individual within this room... There is not one aspect of your reality that you have not already projected before you even engage it. This is creation. This is how it operates... This is what you do without even thinking. You do it automatically, easily... At times you may even be miserable in relation to what you do not want that you created with no effort and no thinking. And you can create what you do want as easily and with as little thinking. It is merely a matter of being aware of what you are doing and paying attention. (Elias, 22 Oct 11)

You are consciousness. The nature of consciousness is expansion. What is expansion? Expansion is more. Your nature, your very nature is to create more, and you do it in every moment, in every day of your existence, whether you are aware of it or not. You are continuously creating more. Therefore, your attention is very important, for your attention is the single most influencing factor in relation to what you create more of... If you are paying attention to how satisfied you are, and how content you are, and how comfortable you are, you will create more of that. If you are paying attention to what you do not have, you will create more lack. (Elias, 15 Mar 13)

There is no such thing as an idle thought. (Jeshua, *WOH*, lesson 3)

You are... eternally a creator. And this is the one thing that you have no free will about. You can never decide to be a non-participant in the very mystery of creation's extension. (Jeshua, *WOH*, lesson 8)

It is much easier to send out ripples and experience them when they come back in a blissful way, a way that brings you peace, joy, fun, laughter, play and unlimitedness, instead of having to constantly butt your head against something that you would rather transmute or run away from. (Jeshua, *WOH*, lesson 9)

You do constantly create, whether you know it or not. The trouble is that you do not know what creations you produce unwittingly. You create with every breath you take, with every thought you think, with every attitude you display. (Pathwork, 9 Feb 73)

It only takes you a moment to envision happiness and your whole body will feel joyful. It only takes you a moment to play the part of a wretched creature whom no one has befriended, and you will feel sorrow and pity for yourself. It only takes a moment to do that. It takes you but a moment to stop weeping and to laugh with glee. It takes you a moment to stop judging and feel the beauty of all things. Now who is doing all of this? You. And while you have had this fancy of creating feelings within your being, has anything around you changed? No. But everything that you are has. (Ramtha, *WB*, chapter 5)

Look to those areas of your life in which you are pleased and have done well. See how emotionally and imaginatively you personally reinforced those beliefs and brought them to physical fruition – realize how naturally and automatically the results appeared. Catch hold of those feelings of accomplishment and understand that you can use the same methods in other areas. (Seth, *NPR*, chapter 4)

You are *always* in the process of *creating*. Every moment, every minute, every day... You are a big creation machine, and you are turning out a new manifestation literally as fast as you can think. (Walsch, *CWG I*, chapter 1)

if you're unhappy with any
part of your life...

what underlying belief must you
hold to be creating it?

We've seen that the reality we experience is formed by our beliefs, not our desires – which is why it's so important to reveal and transform major limiting beliefs, otherwise our best efforts to attract abundance and joy may only produce a sense of frustration and failure. One huge challenge we face is that we tend to keep limiting beliefs that conflict with our desires hidden away because we don't want to face them. For example, we might consciously desire to manifest the perfect partner, but if deep down we've been conditioned since childhood to have low self esteem, and to feel we're not worthy of true love, we'll keep manifesting partners who mirror this underlying belief. Until, that is, we unmask and change it.

Ever since Freud started writing about the unconscious mind, therapies geared to uncovering its contents have proliferated. Increasingly we've come to believe that, apart from attempts at meditation or self-hypnosis, we can't gain control of our lives without the aid of some external agent who will uncover the suppressed fears and beliefs hidden away deep in our subconscious – whether these originated in childhood or in supposed past lives. We'll return to the issue of therapy, and how undue reliance on it can disempower and limit us, in the next chapter. But most of our sources at least hint at the idea that we have far more control than Freud and his varied lines of successors, both conventional and alternative, would have us believe – although it's worth pointing out that one therapeutic approach that to some extent mirrors the advice given in this chapter is cognitive behavioural therapy, or CBT.

Jeshua, the Pathwork Guide and especially Seth go further than the others and explicitly insist that, for most of us, our supposedly hidden beliefs can be accessed by our conscious mind – once we make up our minds and *choose* to unearth them. The latter suggests we should deliberately work through our various beliefs in different areas of our lives, writing them down as we go. He stresses that when doing this we should include those areas where they're serving us well, to act as an example and make sure we don't discourage ourselves by only focusing on those aspects of our lives that are less desirable.

If for whatever reason this technique doesn't produce the desired results, there's another way of approaching any aspect of our life that we find unpleasant or unfulfilling. Because reality is a mirror that only reflects back to us what we're putting out, we can work backwards from the undesirable result we're seeing by asking the simple question: 'What *must* I believe about myself to be creating the reality I'm experiencing?' But Seth indicates that even this process can be complicated by 'core' beliefs that can hide behind the more obvious conflicting ones. These of course take more work to uncover, and involve delving further by asking each time, 'Is there a belief underlying *that*?'

From personal experience we can end up tying ourselves in knots with this, especially if we're having problems in more than one major area of our lives – because then we're trying to work out any linkages between them too. So my best advice would be not to take this to extremes, and to progress one step at a time. Change the most obvious limiting belief, and give it some time to work. Only if that doesn't produce results should you need to delve deeper to find a more fundamental core belief underlying it.

key quotes

The frequency you give off determines the experience you get back, and that then reinforces the belief that originally created that reality experience, and on, and on, and on. It escalates from there, until you break the chain by saying, 'Wait a minute, I created this! I attracted this by what I believe is the strongest, most likely, most possible definition within my belief system structure. Well, is that what I prefer to believe? Yes or no? If no, then what do I prefer to believe?.. I prefer to believe this instead.' Then you recreate a new definition of what you now believe to be true and apply that... and behave as if you believe it. (Bashar, *Fundamentals*)

A creator who understands their infinite power... turns to look upon every moment of their experience that they might discern what choice they must have made to bring about the effects they are currently experiencing. When a bill comes... and there are not enough golden coins in the chequebook to pay for it, the creator *stops...* and begins to wonder, 'What thought must I have dropped into the pool of my mind to create the *effect* of lacking golden coins? And is that a thought I wish to drop into my mind so that I create similar effects in my tomorrows?' (Jeshua, *WOH*, lesson 9)

Every moment of every experience you have ever had is *available* for you, right back to the moment of conception. (Jeshua, *WOT*, lesson 5)

As you go back in time and look at your life, ask: 'What must I have believed previously for this effect to be showing up?' For instance if you have no money, look well at what you have believed about money in the past. Especially look to see: what were the beliefs about money that my parents held?.. [Did they] believe that spirituality and material wealth cannot go together?.. Do you find a block at receiving money for being of service to others, but no block in receiving money for doing something you dislike? (Jeshua, *WOK*, lesson 5)

Often the human mind will say, 'I desire a perfect loving relationship.' But deep in the quiet of the mind is the thought, 'Except I don't deserve it. I'm unlovable...' Therefore, when you desire, look well and watch with subtle vigilance, what *contrary thoughts* seem to also come up in the mind. Then follow those contrary thoughts so that they become crystal clear. (Jeshua, *WOK*, lesson 11)

Often a number of contradictory will currents create a short circuit... but creation continues to go on below the surface. Its products manifest as tangible life experience, and the entity feels at a loss, believing what life brings is totally independent from its own willing and knowing. Any path of genuine development must bring all the confused and contradictory desires to the surface. (Pathwork, 2 Sep 69)

The human condition can best be expressed in a general way by the following three levels of consciousness: the higher self which is the God consciousness; the lower self which is the demonic self; and the mask self which hides the demonic or lower self. Needless to say, there are many degrees and stages within each of these levels of consciousness. The way they overlap, cancel each other out and create confusion, along with the resulting indirect effects and chain reactions, needs to be explored, understood, and mastered. This work is the pathwork. All these aspects of the personality can be conscious or unconscious to varying degrees. The less awareness you have of any of these states, the more conflict exists in your life and the less you are equipped to deal with life, yourself, and other people. Low awareness will also certainly result in your being farther removed from the realization of your ultimate divine self... The aim is to unify these three levels of consciousness so that the mask and lower selves dissolve and only the true higher self manifests and expresses itself. Only when the lower and mask selves are entirely conscious and their exact manifestations understood can misconceptions be corrected. (Pathwork, 24 Sep 71)

When you feel unhappy, sad, angry, fearful, harried, separate – or any other feeling that you do not like – examine your thinking. You will soon see the connection between your thinking – judging yourself or others, or seeing life in facets or dimensions – and your displeasing emotions. And soon, as you tire of these feelings, you will begin to refine your thinking to remove the judgments that separate you from life. (Ramtha, *WB*, chapter 19)

Your ideas and beliefs form the structure of your experience. Your beliefs and the reasons for them can be found in your conscious mind... Your conscious beliefs are extremely important, and you are not at the mercy of events or causes that dwell far beneath your awareness. (Seth, *NPR*, chapter 2)

Examine your physical reality in all of its aspects. Realize that your physical experience and environment is the materialization of your beliefs. If you find great exuberance, health, effective work, abundance, smiles on the faces of those you meet… a world that is good, people that like you, take it for granted again that your beliefs are beneficial. But if you find poor health, a lack of meaningful work, a lack of abundance, a world of sorrow and evil, then assume that your beliefs are faulty and begin examining them. (Seth, *NPR*, chapter 2)

It may be easy for you to see beliefs that are invisible to others in themselves… You may be able to point at friends or acquaintances an see clearly that *their* ideas are invisible beliefs which limit their experience – and yet be blind to your own invisible beliefs. (Seth, *NPR*, chapter 3)

One of the most hampering beliefs of all… is the idea that the clues to current behavior are buried and usually inaccessible. This belief itself closes to you the contents of your own conscious mind and prevents you from looking there for the answers that are available… You have not learned to use your consciousness properly or fully, so that it seems that imagination, emotions and reasoning are separate faculties, or sometimes set against each other. The mature conscious mind, once more, accepts data from the exterior world *and* from the interior one… I am not minimizing the importance of the inner self. All of its infinite resources are placed at the *disposal* of your conscious mind, however, and for your conscious purposes… Proponents of 'conscious-reasoning-mind-above-all' theories advocate a use of intellect and reasoning powers, while not recognizing their source in the inner self… On the other hand there are those who stress the great value of the inner self, the emotional being, at the expense of the conscious mind… Both groups ignore the miraculous unity of the psyche, the fine natural interworkings that exist between the so-called conscious mind and the so-called unconscious – the incredibly rich interaction as each gives and takes. (Seth, *NPR*, chapter 4)

You may be poor. Following my suggestions, you may try to alter the belief and say, 'My wants are taken care of and I have a great abundance.' Yet you may still find yourself unable to meet your bills. Imaginatively you may see the next bill coming, with you unable to pay it. 'I *will* have enough money,' you say. 'This is my new belief.' But nothing changes so you think, 'My conscious thoughts mean nothing.' Yet upon examination of your beliefs you may find a deep conviction of your own unworthiness. You may find yourself thinking, 'I am no one to begin with,' or 'The rich get richer and the poor get poorer,' or 'The world is against me,' or 'Money is wrong. People who have it are not spiritual.' You may discover, again, one of numerous beliefs that all lead to the fact that you do not want to have money or are afraid of it. In any case your imagination and your beliefs go hand in hand. (Seth, *NPR*, chapter 4)

There are two ways to get at your own conscious beliefs. The most direct is to have a series of talks with yourself. Write down your beliefs in a variety of areas, and you will find that your believe different things at different times. Often there will be contradictions readily apparent... Examine the conflicts. Invisible beliefs will appear that will unite those seemingly diverse attitudes. Invisible beliefs are simply those of which you are fully aware but prefer to ignore, because they represent areas of strife which you have not been willing to handle thus far. They are quite available once you are determined to examine the *complete* contents of your conscious mind. If this strikes you as too intellectual a method, then you can also work backward from your emotions to your beliefs. (Seth, *NPR*, chapter 11)

As you examine the contents of your conscious mind, it may seem to you that you hold so many different beliefs at different times that you cannot correlate them. They will, however, form into clear patterns. You will find a grouping of core beliefs about which the others gather. If you think of these as planets, then your other ideas orbit about them. There may be some 'invisible beliefs' and there may be one or two invisible *core* beliefs. These, following the analogy, would be hidden behind the other, brighter, more obvious 'planets', and yet would show their presence through their effects upon your relationships with all of the other visible core beliefs in your 'planetary system'. Questions you cannot seem to answer as you study your own ideas, for example, may lead you to suspect the existence of such invisible core beliefs. Let me emphasize that they *are* consciously available. (Seth, *NPR*, chapter 11)

[Referring to one of the people Jane Roberts helped over the phone] Andrea never doubted the 'fact' that life was more difficult for a woman than for a man. When she examined her beliefs this escaped her. The invisible belief, however, affected her behavior and experience. Now she understands it and can deal with it as a belief, and not as a condition of reality over which she has no control. (Seth, *NPR*, chapter 11)

[As well as unearthing your limiting beliefs] write a list of your abilities and accomplishments... Any talent or achievement should be noted as honestly as you recorded the most minute 'defects' earlier. There is no human being alive who does not have creative abilities in his or her own way... When you catch yourself falling into a mood in which you feel inferior, look at your second list. (Seth, *NPR*, chapter 22)

DON'T SUPPRESS YOUR FEARS AND PAINFUL EMOTIONS, THEY'RE YOUR FRIENDS

This is one area where we see a degree of variation between our sources. At one end of the scale Abraham generally tend more towards the suggestion that when we're feeling negative emotions or thinking negative thoughts we should attempt to replace them with more desirable ones – although their two quotes below do indicate that further reflection may sometimes be required. But the Pathwork Guide, Jeshua and Seth not only propose that we need to pay attention when negative thoughts and emotions arise, they also emphasise that we need to make sure we properly explore them rather than just mask them. The answer to any apparent divergence here is, I suspect, the degree to which the negative thoughts, beliefs or emotions are embedded within the person. Relatively superficial ones can probably be replaced relatively easily, while those with greater intensity and regularity will require closer inspection.

An important piece of advice from Seth – which ties in with his suggestion in the previous chapter that we should question all our values – is that it's healthy not to accept *anything* as a statement of *fact* about ourselves, but merely to see everything as a *belief* that may have no real validity when closely inspected. For example if we believe we're lonely we'll experience that, even if surrounded by hundreds of friends. If we believe we're poor, we'll always squander however much money we have, to produce the believed rather than desired effect. So when investigating our limiting beliefs we should take absolutely nothing for granted.

One other thing that's worth drawing out here is that fears and painful or aggressive emotions nearly always stem from one of two things: an underlying sense of powerlessness, or of inadequacy. We can easily tell how content we are in our skin by how we react when someone is rude or aggressive to us or criticises us, especially if it's a stranger in a situation that comes suddenly and unexpectedly – when we're driving is an obvious example. If we can just ignore it or laugh it off, or even apologise if we think we're in the wrong, we're doing well. If we explode with rage that someone could think we're anything less than perfect and dare to judge us, or if such a simple event leaves a lasting feeling of being useless and worthless, it's a sure sign we've got work to do.

key quotes

Rather than trying to monitor your thoughts, we encourage you to simply pay attention to how you are feeling. For if you should choose a thought that is not in harmony with the way the broader, older, wiser, loving Inner Being part of you sees it, you will feel the discord, and then you can easily redirect your thought to something that feels better and which therefore serves you better. (Abraham, *LOA*, part 2)

Whenever you feel negative emotion, it is always telling you that whatever you are thinking about is important, and that you are thinking the opposite of what you really desire. (Abraham, *LOA*, part 2)

If you are paying attention to the way you are feeling, you will always know whether you are focused upon what you want or upon the lack of it – for when you are thinking of what you want, you are feeling good, and when you are thinking of the lack of what you want, you are feeling bad. (Abraham, *LOA*, part 3)

What is most important when you recognize that you are thinking a negative thought is to, in whatever way you can, stop thinking the negative thought. If there is a belief within you that is very powerful, then you may find that this negative thought will come up again and again and again. And so, you continually have to divert your thought from that negative thought onto something else. In that case, it is of value to recognize the troublesome thought and modify it by applying a new perspective to it. In other words, mould the conflicting belief into one that is not so conflicting – and then it will not keep coming up and haunting you. (Abraham, *LOA*, part 5)

Fear is just a knock at the door: 'Pay attention to this. This is something you want to know about yourself, this is something you need to know to integrate within yourself, to become more of who you are.'(Bashar, *Fundamentals*)

As you go through your day, observe when you feel as though you are in contraction. Are the muscles of the body tight? Is the breath very shallow? Does your voice become faster or louder when you speak about some energy in someone else? That is a sign that you need to do healing within yourself... Therefore, count it as a blessing if you feel disturbed. (Jeshua, *WOH*, lesson 3)

This brings us right to the whole question of what this path is... Dealing with confusions, inner misconceptions, misunderstandings, destructive attitudes, alienating defenses, negative emotions, paralyzed feelings – all this is essential, and all of this psychotherapy also attempts to do. However, while this is the ultimate goal of psychotherapy, the Pathwork enters its most important phase only after this stage is over and done with, and that most important phase is, briefly, the learning of how to activate the greater consciousness dwelling within every human soul... How can you gauge whether or not untruthfulness on a deeper level exists?.. The key is how do you feel about yourself and about your life? How meaningful, fulfilled, and rich is your life? Do you feel secure with others? Do you feel comfortable about yourself, your most intimate self, in the presence of others or at least of some people with whom you have the same goal in common? How much joy are you capable of feeling, giving, and receiving? Are you plagued with resentments, anxiety, and tension, with loneliness and a sense of isolation? Do you need a lot of overactivity in order to alleviate anxiety? Exhilaration, enthusiasm, joyousness, the unique blend of excitement and peace which connotes spiritual wholeness are a result of inner truthfulness. When these states are absent, then truthfulness must be absent. It is as simple as that, my friends. If you expect of this path, indeed demand of your life and therefore of any path you contemplate to enter, to by-pass feeling your anxiety; feeling your pain; owning up to your dishonesties, your cheating, your spitefulness, your games and more or less subtle pretension – which you do not wish to admit and for which you do not want to take responsibility – then you better not start on this path. But if you expect something realistic and are prepared to embark on the journey into yourself, to find, acknowledge, and bring out whatever it is; if you summon all your inner truthfulness and commitment to it, your courage and humility not to appear other than you are (even in your own eyes), then you have indeed every right to expect that this path will help you realize your full life, fulfill your longing in every conceivable way. (Pathwork, 20 Oct 72)

So you who carry your baggage of burdens heavily upon your back, if it makes you happy to do so, so be it. But if you have learned all there is to learn from them and you are tired of them, get rid of them. How? By loving them, embracing them, and allowing them to be in your being. Once you have done that, they shan't ever hold you again. (Ramtha, *WB*, chapter 20)

When you feel the rise of unpleasant emotions, take a moment and make an effort to identify their source. The answers are far more available than you may have previously believed. Accept such feelings as your own in the moment. Do not shove them underneath, ignore them or try to substitute what you think of as good thoughts. First be aware of the reality of your feelings. As you become more aware of your beliefs over a period of time, you will see how they bring forth certain feelings automatically. A man who is sure of himself is *not* angry at every slight done him, nor does he carry grudges. A man who fears for his own worth, however, is furious under such conditions. The free flow of your emotions will always lead you back to your conscious beliefs if you do not impede them. (Seth, *NPR*, chapter 11)

Your emotions will always lead you into a realization of your beliefs if you do not impede them... You are at the mercy of your emotions only when you fear them. They are the motion of your being. They go hand in hand with your intellect. But when you are unaware of the contents of your conscious mind, and not fair with your emotions, you run into difficulty... Any emotion will change into another if you experience it honestly. Otherwise you clog the natural movement of your entire system. Fear, faced and felt with its bodily sensations and the thoughts that go along with it, will automatically bring about its own state of resolution. The conscious system of beliefs behind the impediment will be illuminated, and you will realize that you feel a certain way because you believe an idea that causes and justifies such a reaction. (Seth, *NPR*, chapter 11)

The next time Andrea feels inadequate, for example, she is to actively experience that feeling, realizing that even though she feels inferior this does not mean that she *is* inferior. She is to say, 'I feel inferior,' and at the same time to understand that the feeling is not a statement of fact but of emotion... Experiencing your emotions as such is not the same as accepting them as statements of fact about your own existence... If you deny the validity of the emotion itself, and pretend it away, then you will never be led to question the beliefs behind it. (Seth, *NPR*, chapter 11)

You must accept the validity of your feelings while realizing that they... are not necessarily factual statements of your reality... You might be an excellent mother while feeling that you are very inadequate. You may be most successful in reaching your goals while still thinking yourself a failure. By recognizing these differences and honestly following the feelings through... you will be led to the beliefs behind them. A series of self-revelations will inevitably result. (Seth, *NPR*, chapter 11)

An individual who thinks that he is poor will lose or misuse, or badly invest, any amount of money, whether he works hard for it or is given it. A person who has hypnotized himself into a state of loneliness will be desolate although surrounded by a hundred friends and admirers. (Seth, *NPR*, chapter 16)

If you hate a parent... you cannot use the point of power to tell yourself that you love the parent instead. [You need to] understand the reasons for the hate... You have been told to experience your feelings and not to deny them, so you are not to use the point of power as an attempt to refute the reality of your emotions at any given time... Each of you must work from the point of your own reality. There is no other way. Period. If you feel filled with rage, then do not say, 'I am filled with peace,' and expect results. You will only be blanketing your feelings and inhibiting your energy and power. If you are furious, then beat a pillow and experience the rage, but without violence to another. Work it through until you are physically exhausted. If you do this honestly, the reasons for the fury will come to you, and they will often be quite obvious. You simply did not want to face them. In almost all cases of this kind, your feelings will represent a sense of powerlessness on your part, where you delegated strength to a situation or individual and felt your effort futile in contrast. Then use the point of power and feel the energy of your own being surge through your experience. The knowledge of your own power releases you from all fears, and hence from all rage... [Then] as you trust yourself more you will naturally express your feelings, and their suppression will not bring about explosive reactions any more. They will come and go. (Seth, *NPR*, chapter 17)

What you look at disappears. That is, it ceases to have its illusory form. You see it for what it is. (Walsch, *CWG III*, chapter 8)

THERE'S NO SUCH THING AS FAILURE, THERE'S ONLY EXPERIENCE

You may have heard phrases such as 'failure is only feedback'. In a similar vein Abraham suggests that everything we experience is just data that allows us to refine what we do want and don't want in our lives. Meanwhile Jeshua proposes that nothing we do is a failure because everything has contributed to who we are, and any judgment of ourselves is just as damaging as judgment of others – perhaps more so. He also tells us that the most helpful thing we can do is look at *all* our creations with the innocence of a child. What's more if we can do that when we're right in the middle of what we'd normally perceive as serious suffering, *then* we've really started to move into mastery.

key quotes

Most of your time will be spent collecting data – data that will help you decide what it is you want. (Abraham, LOA, part 2)

In reality, failure is not even remotely possible... All events in space and time – everything you experience – are perfectly neutral... The only failure seems to occur when within your own consciousness you believe that it is not acceptable to receive and own and embrace your creation with love and with innocence. (Jeshua, *WOH*, lesson 2)

You know the experience when things are going well, you are singing a happy tune, and life seems to be moving ahead? Imagine that same quality of trust, faith, and certainty of purpose, even when the buildings are crumbling around you and the bank account has gone dry. Imagine being able to look at those events with the same sense of innocence and wonder with which you would look into the eyes of your beloved... Become again as a little child to enter the kingdom. (Jeshua, *WOH*, lesson 2)

Bringing your attention to the effects you create is a pathway to great freedom. What you did in the past to create the effects that you no longer want was not a sin or a mistake. It was merely a free choice in order to create experience. Fine, you have been there; you have done that. Now, bring love and appreciation to the very effects that you may be judging... In fact, every time you think you have failed, celebrate! Celebrate your so-called failure as though it were a success. For remember it is up to *you* to decide what you will perceive. Events are just neutral... Any successful person knows that they never fail. They merely learn and become wiser. (Jeshua, *WOK*, lesson 5)

Great freedom can come when in the midst of something that you feel to be great suffering, you choose to laugh and say, 'Look at this one! What an amazing script I have written here. I ought to win the Oscar. Who could have done this one better than this?' And, rest assured, you are speaking to one who had some experience at writing rather interesting scripts of suffering. (Jeshua, *WOK*, lesson 11)

Always be very careful that you do not judge what is occurring. For that is the fault that people fall into, saying, 'Why did I call this to myself? This is a horrible experience. Why, oh why did I want this?' All of that is judgment and not gratitude. (Jeshua, *WOK*, lesson 11)

TO CHANGE A DOMINANT BELIEF, RESET YOUR PERCEPTION AND INFORMATION FILTERS

This sort of approach is particularly integral to CBT and it's based on the premise that, once we allow a dominant belief to develop, we're incredibly good at being selective with what we choose to notice in our lives. Specifically we tend to only pay attention to those experiences that reinforce the dominant belief, ignoring those that contradict it. We further reinforce it by selectively searching through our memory banks, again only picking out experiences that support the dominant view.

The trick is, of course, to completely reverse this process. As a simple example, if we feel lonely and isolated, instead of noticing all the times that people ignore us and fail to smile and say 'hello', we should focus on those people who *do* notice us and *are* friendly. They may be few and far between to start with, but the more we do this the more they'll come to dominate our experience. What's more, if we really decide to take the bull by the horns we can be proactive and say 'hello' and smile *first*. Suddenly we'll find that most of those people who would otherwise have walked on by, wrapped up in their own world, talking into their mobile phone or whatever, will respond in kind. In fact most of them probably feel exactly the same *as we once used to*, and will really appreciate the effort we've made.

key quotes

Allowing is the art of finding a way of looking at things that still allows your connection to your Inner Being at the same time. It is achieved by selectively sifting through the data of your time-space reality and focusing upon things that feel good. (Abraham, *LOA*, part 4)

To be an *Allower*... means that you are able to see, and therefore solicit forth, from the universe, from your world, and from your friends, that which is in harmony with you, while you let the other parts go unnoticed by you – therefore unattracted by you, and therefore not invited by you. (Abraham, *LOA*, part 4)

Every hurt that you have ever known is like a cloud that began to pass into the field of your awareness because you perceived things in a certain way. If that hurt is still lodged within you, it is because you latched on to it. You followed the voice of ego, which caused you to believe that you are identified with that feeling, with that perception... Your knuckles are white, trying to hold on to limitation and guilt, to unworthiness and doubt. (Jeshua, *WOH*, lesson 2)

Your day is chock full of opportunities to discover a deeper truth... the freedom within you to choose what you want to perceive and to elicit only what you want to feel. (Jeshua, *WOH*, lesson 3)

You will learn to be careful what thoughts you think without either repressing or suppressing undesirable and destructive thoughts. This [latter] does not help. You will learn to deal with such material, to challenge its accuracy and be open for other alternatives. Learn to understand what it is in you that makes you want to think that way and what price you pay. Begin to see creation as the relationship between the causes and effects that you have always seen as unrelated. (Pathwork, 9 Feb 73)

You collect from the physical universe, and the interior one, data that seems to correlate with your beliefs. (Seth, *NPR*, chapter 3)

Which you? Which world? If you are lonely it is because you believe in your loneliness in this present point that you acknowledge as time. From what seems to be the past you draw only those memories that reinforce your condition and you project those into the future... One person may... begin to doubt his ability to get along with others. So he may begin to look into his past – *with that belief in mind*, that he cannot relate – and then find within previous conduct all kinds of reasons to support the idea. If he journeyed through his memories trying to find a different kind of proof instead, then in that same past he would discover instances when he did relate well with others. Your present beliefs structure the memories which will parade before you now – *and what you remember will then seem to justify the beliefs*. When you are trying to alter your beliefs, look through your past with the new conceptions in mind. If you are ill, remember when you were not. Search your life for proofs of your health. (Seth, *NPR*, chapter 15)

If you constantly focus on the belief that your early background was damaging and negative, then only such experiences will flow into your present life from the past. It does no good to say, 'But my life *was* traumatic,' therefore reinforcing the belief. You must in one way or another modify that conviction, or preferably change it entirely – or you will never escape from its effects. This does not mean 'lying' to yourself; but if it seems to you that your background held *no* joys, accomplishments or pleasures, then you are lying to yourself now. You have concentrated on the negative to such a degree that anything else seems invisible. From the present you have hypnotized yourself, viewing the past not as it was to your experience, but as it appears now in the light of your current beliefs. (Seth, *NPR*, chapter 15)

YOU CAN CHANGE IF YOU WANT TO, BY CHANGING YOUR THINKING

How often do we hear the mantra, 'that's just how I am'? Do you ever say that about yourself? Well, guess what? That statement is *never, ever* true – unless of course you *choose* to make it so. And it *is* a choice. Any of us can be anything we want to be. The sky's the limit, as we'll see in the final chapter.

Again I'll use myself to provide a simple example. I'm an ex-smoker – in fact a 'smokaholic' in that, although I gave up over five years ago, if I just had one I'd be back on them again full time. For the last few years I was on fifty or sixty a day. That's a proper habit. Was it difficult to stop? *No!* It was as easy as taking candy from a baby. I didn't need patches or electronic replacements or whatever. Why? Because I'd started to cough sufficiently, all day, every day, that I just *knew* if I carried on I'd only have a few years left. So I only had to ask myself a simple question: do I *choose* to die relatively early, or do I *choose* to carry on for some years yet because I've got things I'd still like to achieve? I chose the latter, and after that it was easy. What's more, I *know* that every day my lungs get that little bit cleaner and that little bit stronger.

Change – even major change – really is very simple if you *desire* it enough and *believe* it's possible. Nor does it have to take a long time. It can be instantaneous. Once I *really* made that decision, for the first time in my life when giving up I didn't miss cigarettes. The change was actually instant.

Of course most changes take a little longer to become fully embedded, and in this context it's interesting to note that neuroscientists have now proved conclusively that merely imagining something activates exactly the same parts of the brain that would be activated if we were actually experiencing it. What is more, if we consistently and repeatedly imagine that something, we create new neural pathways that in turn create a whole new set of conditioned responses. In other words modern science backs up the idea that we can change if we choose to.

Having said that it's time now to return to the intensely difficult situation of someone in a deep rut, perhaps with major problems in several areas of their life, who's trying to claw their way out. As mentioned briefly in the Preface I've been there, and I know what it's like. The advice to 'change your thinking', while absolutely correct, is so much easier to say than do when you've created *such* a downward spiral that it feels as though your life lies in tatters around you. Our projection into this reality may be a play that's not to be taken too seriously, but when you're plumbing the depths it can be hugely difficult to regain that perspective.

If anyone reading this is in a similar situation, I hope the quotes in this section will give you the confidence that you *can* turn things around. As to specifics, almost certainly you'll have allowed your inner victim to take serious control over your thought processes. The problem is this may *not* be obvious, because if you're like me you'll still be trying all the ways you can think of to be positive and create more desirable outcomes. But until you expose that inner victim these will most likely come to nothing. Having said that, the mere act of exposure may be sufficient. It was for me. As soon as I realised what I'd been doing I literally declared *'No more victim!'* and that was enough to start to turn the ship around. But even then you may not want to try and resolve everything at once. Pick the area of your life that you feel most confident about changing, and start with that.

key quotes

It is our desire to help you understand that you can get to wherever you want to be from wherever you are, no matter where you are or what your current state of being... In order to effect true positive change in your experience, you must disregard how things are – as well as how others are seeing you – and give more of your attention to the way you prefer things to be... You would not likely see a sculptor throwing his large wad of clay down onto his worktable exclaiming, 'Oh, it didn't turn out right!' He knows that he must put his hands into the clay and work with it to mould it so that the vision in his mind matches the clay on his table. The variety of your life experience gives you the clay from which you will mould your life experience, and merely observing it as it is, without getting a hold of it and deliberately molding it to match your desires, is not satisfying – and is not what you had in mind when you made the decision to come into this time-space reality. We want you to understand that your 'clay', no matter how it may look right now, is moldable. No exceptions. (Abraham, *LOA*, part 2)

Take your attention from that which does *not* please you, put your attention upon that which *does* please you, and you will then change the momentum. Not instantly, but it will begin to change. (Abraham, *LOA*, part 4)

It takes a very strong being to take your thought from what is not wanted when it is that intense. In other words, when your toe is really throbbing, it is difficult to put your thought upon a healthy foot. In extremely negative situations, we would suggest distraction rather than trying to change the thought. In other words, go to sleep or go to a movie; listen to music; pet your cat. (Abraham, *LOA*, part 3)

A habit is something you do that you don't know you're doing. Once you know you're doing it, you don't have it anymore, it's gone. If you appear to keep doing it, it's because for some reason you choose to. 'Ooh, responsibility, oh no, responsibility, you mean I have to take responsibility for the fact that I keep doing this, I can't just foist it off on the idea that it's a habit as an excuse?' Nope. Not once you know you have the habit!.. So when you know you have a habit, that does not mean that it's the beginning of the process of changing it, it means it's the end, you don't have it anymore. Now, if you keep appearing to do it, it's because you have a definition of the habit that says, 'This is difficult. Now that I'm aware of it I have to go through some lengthy process full of struggle and effort, in order to divest myself of this horribly difficult behavior pattern. I know this is just going to take years and years and years!' Well, ask yourself at that moment, what would you be getting out of it to allow it to take so long? How is it serving you to procrastinate?.. So take responsibility, demand responsibility, insist on responsibility. Believe me, it's the most fun! Because when you take responsibility you are at choice, you are self-empowered, you know you have the ability to choose and you are free to choose. That's freedom. That's self empowerment. (Bashar, *Fundamentals*)

[Using symbolism of dropping new pebbles in the pool of

consciousness] 'I see what I have carried along with me. Well, it was fun. I gained a few things. Now, what's next? Unlimitedness – kerplunk! Perfect love – kerplunk! Wealth – kerplunk! The ability to heal – kerplunk! kerplunk! kerplunk! (Jeshua, *WOH*, lesson 8)

Let us take the example that you are convinced you can experience only this or that negative manifestation in life. Once you observe the tenacity with which you take this for granted in any given area of your life experience, you can ask the question, 'Does it really have to be so?' The moment this question is raised, you begin to open a crack in the door. (Pathwork, 2 Sep 69)

Visualize the boundaries of your mind by questioning yourself about all the things that you think are impossible for you. Where you are hopeless and frightened there must be an idea of finiteness that is simply locked in your mind... It is therefore necessary that you begin to puncture that closed circuit... You do this by first making it known to yourself that you do hold limited beliefs, instead of unquestioningly taking them for granted. The next step is to challenge them. This requires taking the trouble to walk through in the well-practiced attitude of self-observation and self-confrontation your limited beliefs and to truly think about them. (Pathwork, 23 Oct 74)

This plane is the plane of creative realities. Whatever truth you create in your life, know that you also can change. What allows you to become sovereign is to know that you can do and become anything you want and that you have the ability to change your mind any time you want. (Ramtha, *WB*, chapter 12)

The 'story of your life' is written by you... You are the author. There is no reason, therefore, for you to view the drama and feel trapped by it. The power to change your own condition is your own. You only have to exercise it. (Seth, *SS*, Appendix)

If you are in poor health, you can remedy it. If your personal relationships are unsatisfactory, you can change them for the better. If you are in poverty, you can instead find yourself surrounded by abundance. (Seth, *NPR*, Preface)

The exterior appearance is a replica of inner desire. You can change your personal world. You do change it without knowing it. You have only to use your ability consciously, to examine the nature of your thoughts and feelings and project those with which you basically agree. (Seth, *NPR*, Preface)

You must be convinced that you can alter your beliefs. You must be willing to try. Think of a limiting idea as a muddy color and your life as a multidimensional painting that is marred. You change the idea as an artist would change his palette... If you think that limiting thoughts are a portion of you, permanently attached therefore, you will not think of washing them off. You would behave instead like a mad artist who says, 'My paints are a part of me. They have stained my fingers, and there is nothing I can do about it.' (Seth, *NPR*, chapter 2)

Think of your own beliefs as furniture that can be rearranged, changed, renewed, completely discarded or replaced. Your ideas are yours. They should not control you. It is up to you to accept those that you choose to accept. (Seth, *NPR*, chapter 3)

There is no need for undesirable aspects of your contemporary reality to be projected into the future, unless you use the power of the present to do so. If you learn to get hold of this feeling of power now, you can use it most effectively to alter your life situation in whatever way you choose. (Seth, *NPR*, chapter 15)

You love the grief, you love the drama. That is, until you don't anymore. There comes a certain point in your evolution when you cease to love the drama, cease to love the 'story' as you've been living it. That's when you decide – actively choose – to change it. Only most don't know how. You now do. To change your reality, simply *stop thinking like that*. (Walsch, *CWG I*, chapter 12)

If [the soul] does not like what it is experiencing, or wishes a different experience for any reason, it simply conceives of a *new* experience of self, and, quite literally, *changes its mind.* (Walsch, *CWG I*, chapter 13)

Your perspective creates your thoughts… Assume a different perspective and you will have a different thought about everything. In this way you will have learned to control your thought, and, in the creation of your experience, controlled thought is everything. (Walsch, *CWG III*, chapter 3)

don't look outside yourself
for answers...

because the best person
to help you is you

We saw in the last chapter that, for most of us, everything we need to know and work on that may be limiting our ability to attract a life of joy and abundance is available to our *conscious* mind – if only we're prepared to open it up fully, be honest with ourselves, and not hide certain beliefs and feelings away as being too painful to examine.

This chapter picks up from that and reinforces the message that each of us is the best person to help *ourself*. Too many of us spend most of our lives running away from ourselves in one way or another. Some hide behind a succession of unsatisfactory and unfulfilling relationships. Some immerse themselves in work, and in amassing money and possessions, so others will give them the praise they crave – all of which somehow never satisfies them. Some exhaust themselves trying to help others, brushing over the help their *own* inner self is crying out for. Some travel the world searching for enlightenment, ignoring the fact that the *only* place they'll ever find it in any true and lasting form is *within*.

We human beings, including – perhaps even especially – spiritual seekers, have a tendency to behave like sheep. Many seem to need to have a guru of some sort to follow, even if they change them regularly. It really is time we grew up. It's fine to read books and attend lectures or workshops, and take from them whatever we can. But we should all proclaim ourselves as *our own guru*. Starting now. Only then will we begin to really learn anything that's worth knowing about who we are as individuals – which is what we all are – and what each of us is really doing here. An integral aspect of this is that we have to learn to love ourselves properly, indeed to love ourselves more than we love anyone else. This advice should by now make perfect sense in the context of the material we've already covered, and because quotes about it are ubiquitous I've included only a couple from our sources.

key quotes

[The Way of Mastery] is a way unknown to many that would call themselves spiritual teachers. For it is not a way of resting on or becoming dependent on magical means. It is, rather, the pathway which cultivates within you the decision to turn your attention upon your own mind, upon your own behavior, upon what is true and real for you moment to moment... To constantly retrain the mind so that it assumes complete responsibility in each moment... You need to come to the point where you say to yourself, 'I have done this to myself. I did it; I must correct it. No one is to blame. The world is innocent.' (Jeshua, *WOH*, lesson 1)

So many of you upon your physical plane keep searching for some kind of magic that will bring the kingdom of heaven to you. You cannot bring it *to you*. You can only become aware of how you are using it to create the ripples that you send out *from yourself*. (Jeshua, *WOH*, lesson 9)

There are many in your world who would yet perceive spirituality as a way to get out of the place in which they find themselves, not understanding that they can be nowhere save than in their own mind. (Jeshua, *WOT*, lesson 8)

If you... want to attract beings who will support you and love you, decide to be a being who supports and loves *yourself*... If you start to go through a single day, and you notice that by five o'clock your energy field is not feeling very good, ask yourself: 'Where have I been waiting for love to show up as a gift of something or someone else to me?' Stop what you are doing and be the one who gives love to *yourself* – simply so that you can enjoy it. (Jeshua, *WOK*, lesson 4)

There are many methods and practices that attempt to attain realization of the spiritual self. However, many of them, though using valid methods to forcefully reach the goal, don't pay sufficient attention to those areas of the ego self which are steeped in negativity and destructiveness. Success thus achieved is always short-lived and really an illusion even though some of the experiences may be genuine enough... This path will help you realize your full life... Little by little, you will begin to function from your innermost centre, which is a very different experience than the functioning from your periphery, which you are now so accustomed to that you cannot even imagine how else it could be. Now you are constantly dependent on what happens around you. You depend on appreciation and approval by others, on being loved, and on being successful in terms of the world outside you... When you function from your centre, your security and joy spring from a deep well within... In reality, through functioning from your liberated centre, your innermost self, you attract all the abundance of life to you, but you do not depend on it. It enriches you, it is a fulfillment of a legitimate need, but it is not the substance of life. The substance is within... Very, very few people on this earth are willing to undertake this path... They do not wish to take a chance on themselves, on finding the way through their own darkness. But those who have the courage to go all the way, relentlessly and patiently, what glory awaits them in their innermost centre! (Pathwork, 20 Oct 72)

Those of you who desire to follow and worship, or to do more outside of yourselves than within yourselves, I wish you to know that I am not what you are searching for. I am here to help you become sovereign in your own truth, in your own understanding. As long as you serve or worship or devote yourselves to anything outside of yourselves, you will never express the sublime beauty that you are, nor will you ever become truly free. Only you can be your greatest lover. Only you can be your greatest friend and teacher. There is no voice that will ever teach you greater than your own. There is no word written that will ever teach you greater than your own. Who you are this day is the answer to everything you have ever wanted. But if you insist on looking outside of yourselves for paths to follow and entities to worship, you will never truly see or know the glory of God. You can only realize your divinity, your enlightenment, your unfoldment through yourself and your proclaimed love of self. The only way to peace and happiness and fulfillment in your life is to worship and love yourself – for that is loving God – and to love yourself greater than anyone else, for that is what will give you the love and steadfastness to embrace the whole of humanity. (Ramtha, *WB*, chapter 3)

There are more wonders to perceive through this inward exploration than you can possibly believe until you begin such a journey for yourself. (Seth, *SS*, chapter 6)

I would like, therefore, to introduce you to yourself. You will not find yourself by running from teacher to teacher, from book to book. You will not meet yourself through following any particular specialized method of meditation. Only by looking quietly within the self that you know can your reality be experienced, with those connections that exist between the present or immediate self and the inner identity that is multidimensional. (Seth, *SS*, chapter 22)

Many people look to those outside themselves – psychics, doctors, psychiatrists, priests, ministers, friends – for the answers to overall life situations, and in so doing they deny their own abilities of self-understanding and growth... You must begin to trust yourself some time. I suggest you do it now. If you do not then you will forever be looking to others to prove your own merit to you, and you will never be satisfied... Do not place the words of gurus, ministers, priests, scientists, psychologists, friends – or my words – higher than the feelings of your own being. You can learn much from others, but the deepest knowledge must come from within yourself. Your own consciousness is embarked upon a reality that basically can be experienced by no other, that is unique and untranslatable, with its own meaning, following its own paths of becoming. (Seth, *NPR*, chapter 22)

DON'T OVER-RELY ON REGRESSION AND OTHER THERAPIES

One of the most popular spiritual therapies, which normally involves using a specialist to take us back into the past – whether in this life or apparently previous ones – is of course regression. As someone trained in this discipline myself I've seen just how well it can work, particularly in the hands of some of my rather more skilled colleagues. What's more it doesn't rely on the client or even the therapist believing that any past lives that come up are 'real'. Sometimes it's easier for someone to heal painful and unresolved emotions in this life by using similar circumstances in an apparently different life, because they appear more remote. Under our new model this could be that of a resonant soul, but it could equally be a mere placebo concocted using their imagination alone.

Nevertheless, whereas at one time I'd recommend regression therapy almost as a first resort, I now see it as something that should perhaps be used rather more selectively and sparingly. A majority of our sources take this line, emphasising that it's facing up to who we are *now*, and taking full responsibility for that, which really matters. Any attempt to use regression as a way of avoiding ourselves in the present might bring temporary relief, but it's unlikely to be permanent.

This view is of course backed up by our new model, which tells us that resonant souls are responsible for their *own* lives, which are still ongoing, while we're only responsible for this one we're experiencing now. Some linkages might be usefully explored for perspective or contrast. But any suggestion that any problem has its entire roots in a different life, and can be eliminated by revisiting that life – without a close exploration of how and why that same problem is affecting the person in their life *right now* – would merely bypass it. As we've seen in a previous chapter it would be similarly unhelpful to regard any sort of karma as being passed from one life to the next. So if you're going to visit a regression therapist, finding one that guarantees to concentrate at least as much on where you are right now as they do on the past will be important.

As usual, though, the fundamental message of our sources is, 'Don't waste your attention looking back'. They tell us to concentrate on where we are now, and not to pass responsibility for that to a therapist or to another life in the hope of a miracle cure that doesn't exist. They tell us not to give our incredible power away, but to use it not just to create whatever we desire but, as a first priority, to heal ourselves too.

What, then, about looking to the *future*? There's no harm – in fact it can be a seriously useful exercise – to visualise a future *in this life* that's full of abundance and joy. This is one of the tools we can use *ourselves* to create that future now, and any good regression therapist will use 'future pacing' to achieve a similar result. However when we come to the increasingly popular phenomenon of *pro*gression into an apparently future and *different* life, the same issues arise as with past lives. These aren't 'our' lives in any meaningful sense, and they're certainly not our responsibility. They're the responsibility of the soul who's *already* living them. So again if anyone is going to use this therapy they should make sure it doesn't detract from the fact that our focus needs to be on creating *our own* unique experience *now*.

Another therapy that's often combined with regression is 'spirit release', whereby what purport to be separate entities – usually deceased humans – are assumed to have formed a greater or lesser degree of 'attachment' to the living person in question. I don't say this is impossible, although quite how it logically fits with the idea that all lives are simultaneous and ongoing I can't explain. What surely must be said, though, is that any suggestion that such behaviour is widespread, or that it could have a seriously limiting impact on any given individual, would completely detract from the fundamental principle that we all have complete free will and responsibility for creating our own experiences from moment to moment. What's more, as several of our sources suggest, this is an even more obvious way of avoiding responsibility for unhelpful or disruptive behaviours, which are far more likely to reside entirely in our own psyche. Acting as a placebo such therapy may provide some respite, but again permanent resolution would be improbable. By contrast the release of 'trapped' spirits that aren't attached to a human being so much as to a particular location would be a quite different and probably constructive undertaking.

For what it's worth, in the appendix to *Supersoul* I discuss in some detail how I now view my own experiences of victimhood, and of regression and spirit release, in the light of the implications of the new model – and how I myself used the old model of past lives, life plans and spirit attachments as a way of avoiding responsibility in the now. What's more let me reiterate what I said in the previous chapter. As soon as I finally unearthed my own inner victim and the huge part he'd been playing in my life for several years, I needed no therapy. All I had to do was make a firm and committed decision, in the now, to say *'No more victim!'* – and I've stuck to that, in each moment of now, especially in those where he's tried to raise his ugly head again, ever since. That's where the real power lies.

One other refrain that's extremely popular in contemporary spiritual circles is that we're always 'peeling away new layers of the onion'. In other words, if we ever think we've reached a point where there's no more work to do on ourselves, we're likely to receive a rude awakening. Again I don't necessarily say this is wrong at all. But what I would say is that this kind of approach can sometimes keep us almost in a state of bondage to therapy and self improvement, always striving – even *expecting* – to find something new to work on. So if there's any sense in which this stops us from relaxing and loving who we are *right now*, warts and all, and from enjoying the abundance we have *right now*, then arguably this strays into being more of a limiting than an expansive belief.

key quotes

Rather than trying so hard to erase the past, focus on the present. Give thought to what you *now* want. (Abraham, *LOA*, part 3)

Just as now you are that which you are as a culmination of all that you have lived, there is little value for you to sit here and talk about the things you did when you were 3 or 10 or 12. Of course, you are that which you now are *because* of all that – but to continue to look back into your past and regurgitate those experiences does not add much unto that which you are now. (Abraham, *LOA*, part 4)

Many times within physical focus, individuals may draw themselves to an awareness of another focus of essence which experiences a similar quality of energy... This to a point may be beneficial... But there is also a crossing over that certain point in which you... merely perpetuate issues that you create in this focus... You may hold what you may term to be an irrational fear in this focus of water... In this situation, you may be investigating of another focus and allowing yourself to be recognizing that another focus may hold an experience objectively that is influencing in the area of creating a fear of water. Now; as you recognize that this is not your experience... this shall provide you the opportunity to move beyond this fear... which requires no thought process. Merely the recognition itself shall be reconfiguring the energy. Now; conversely, you may be experiencing an element of fearfulness within this focus that you have created through experiences that you have offered to yourself in this focus. These are your creations and your choices. You may also be connecting with another focus which creates similar experiences. This type of a recognition may be quite empowering to you in this focus, as you allow yourself to recognize that you hold the ability to be moving through this issue regardless of the choice of another focus, which may choose to be continuing within that particular creation of fear. But you may also create a type of trap... for yourself in delving... into that focus intensely, for that action merely reinforces what you are creating in this focus. (Elias, 5 Nov 99)

I have found that many of those who consider this life to be mundane or unfeeling often revel in the past, for they see that perhaps the past holds for them a vibrancy of life or the esteem they feel they are lacking. And they fantasize about their past in a most romantic, heroic fashion, for when life here is dull and boring, they can always conclude that they were very heroic in battle and left many women behind weeping for them. And when they did return, the whole town turned out in a celebration that lasted for eons. Or they were more beautiful than any woman in the world at that particular time and had every man as a lover in those days. Now I will tell you this for all to understand. You have all lived many lives, and those lives have been illustrious and romantic, wretched and barbaric, famous and infamous. But all that you were in your past is not as grand as you are now. In this Now, you are the greatest you have ever been, for you are the cumulative knowledge and experience of all the lives you have ever lived. The Now is the purpose for all that was. (Ramtha, *WB*, chapter 16)

It is unwise to look to who you were in your past. When you look to your past for answers, you will never experience this moment of life and the answers that it holds for your future, for you will be too busy with your head backwards to see the Now when it comes. You are curious about who you have been before, yet you don't even know who you are now. (Ramtha, *WB*, chapter 16)

It is not necessary that you learn about your own past lives, though it may be helpful if you understand that you chose the circumstances of your birth *this* time... Knowing your reincarnational background, but not knowing the true nature of your present self, is useless. (Seth, *SS*, chapter 12)

Often psychoanalysis is simply a game of hide-and-seek, in which you continue to relinquish responsibility for your actions and reality and assign the basic cause to some area of the psyche, hidden in a dark forest of the past. Then you give yourself the task of finding this secret. In so doing you never think of looking for it in the conscious mind, since you are convinced that all deep answers lie far beneath – and, moreover, that your consciousness is not only unable to help you but will often send up camouflages instead. So you play that game. (Seth, *NPR*, chapter 2)

[Referring to a secondary personality of another person Jane Roberts' helped over the phone] In spiritualistic circles he would most certainly be interpreted as an evil spirit... Easier to face, often, is the idea that the responsibility for such ideas must belong to another entity or being. (Seth, *NPR*, chapter 6)

You are a multidimensional personality, and within you lies all the knowledge about yourself, your challenges and problems, that you will ever need to know. Others can help you in their own way, and at certain levels of development such help is necessary and good. But my mission is to remind you of the incredible power of your own being, and to encourage you to recognize and use it. (Seth, *NPR*, chapter 8)

It is only because you believe that the ego is such a stepchild of the self that you go to such great lengths to bring out inner knowledge. It is just because individuals are not aware of the resiliency of their own consciousness that they agree to such proceedings. So patient and therapist share the belief that the conscious mind does not have easy access to the needed knowledge... and is unable to handle very intuitive or psychic material. Your beliefs alone make this so... It is because you do not trust your own basic therapeutic nature, or really understand the conscious or unconscious mind, that you run to so many therapies that originate from without the self. (Seth, *NPR*, chapter 10)

When you try 'psychic' experiments you may believe that you are possessed. Your feelings, the repressed ones, will seem demonic. You will be afraid to assign them to yourself, and so will think that they belong to a disembodied spirit. (Seth, *NPR*, chapter 22)

BE CAREFUL OF TOOLS THAT GIVE YOUR POWER AWAY

I've no wish to denigrate those who retain a strong belief in regression therapy. My aim is merely to point out how our sources view it, and how this is inescapably reinforced by the logical implications of our new model. The same goes for a whole host of other tools that we put varying degrees of faith in, which involve placing reliance on someone or something outside ourselves.

If we start with tools such as ritual magic or witchcraft then, just as with karma, they'll invariably prove effective if we believe in them sufficiently. What's more any magical entities will, if enough people place their creative power behind them, take on an independent existence of their own. To the extent that all the ritual and ceremony is merely a way of intensifying our belief in the creative process, it's probably fine if a little over-elaborate. But if undue reliance on such tools strays into acting as a limitation on our creative power, then perhaps they start to become more of a hindrance than a help.

Turning now to those that involve some element of divination – such as astrology, fortune-telling, channelling of personal information, the tarot, I-Ching and so on – again their forecasts will invariably prove accurate and self-fulfilling if the subject believes in them enough. On the plus side one could argue that a positive forecast about meeting a potential new partner, for example, might help someone to have more abundance, because their belief that it's somehow 'ordained' might prove far greater than their belief in their own creative powers. But, of course, forecasts aren't always of the positive variety, and then they can act as a severe limitation.

To fail to appreciate the creative powers we've been endowed with, and instead to attribute them to someone or something else, is to undervalue ourselves and to give our power away. So it's not difficult to argue that all our sources would agree with the sentiments expressed here, precisely because of the primacy they place upon our free will and creative power. Nevertheless, in all the considerable amount of material I went through in my research for this book, I found only one quote that explicitly discusses this topic, and it's from Ramtha.

Because astrology is so popular I might add that Seth enters into a detailed discussion of it in volume two of his *Unknown*

Reality. But it's extremely complex, in one place supporting Ramtha's view, in another seeming to support astrology as having some value but perhaps not in a personal context. Above all most of it isn't immediately relevant to our theme here.

key quotes

Those who practice astrology are indeed beautiful in their true concern for others and their desire to help them. And to study the stars is a wonderful thing, for they are beautiful in their movement and enchanting in their mystery. But if you base your life upon them you are no greater than the gases that make them up... Man has always looked outside of himself to find answers and reasons for his fate and his destiny. It has always been more comforting to blame the silent stars or the rule of kings or the will of God than to look within to the creator of the universes. It has always been easier to seek out priests and prophets and seers for guidance than to believe that oneself is wise enough to be the giver of it. As long as you look outside of yourself for reasons and answers, you will never hear the voice within you, the giver of all truth and the creator of all that is. You will always be at the hands of superstitious beliefs and outrageous reasonings that blind you to the awesome power and infinite understanding that you truly possess... When you are playing with your games, remember who created them. And remember that the same creator, who can become vulnerable to anything he wishes to, can in a moment change whatever he does not like and once again take hold of his life. (Ramtha, *WB*, chapter 12)

BE CAREFUL OF TOOLS THAT TRY TO BYPASS YOUR CONSCIOUS MIND

Let's now turn to what may prove to be an even more contentious area for those who've been brought up in an environment where hallucinogens or psychedelics – there's always debate about the best term to use – are assumed to provide a gateway to discovering the true spiritual self. Again from the research I conducted I only found brief references to this from the Pathwork Guide, but as so often much more comes from Seth, and he's pretty scathing. I find their views interesting and, having had some small degree of experience of 'plant medicine' myself, I'm in partial – although perhaps not full – agreement.

Their argument follows their equally radical view, already discussed in the previous chapter, that our *conscious* mind holds the key to everything we need to know about ourselves, if only we'd be more honest with ourselves and make better use of it. But, of course, nothing scrambles the normal conscious mind more than the use of hallucinogens. Admittedly different people have hugely different reactions to them, and even one person can have hugely different reactions to the same medicine at different times. Some have what they feel to be incredibly transformative and positive 'journeys' – and having seen their reaction, and felt the love and wonder radiating from them, the last thing I'd want to do is denigrate their experience. But what I can say is that if the taking of such medicines becomes a crutch, and especially if responsibility for our lives is to some extent handed over, for example to any sort of god or goddess of the plant involved, then arguably it again becomes more of a limiting than an expansive way of operating.

key quotes

This is the state of being lost which many individuals wish to cure by some magic – drugs, pills, formulas, or even meditation. They also turn to therapies that encourage the helpless state of sickness and overlook the potent factor of their own will which must be used provided it is rightly understood and applied. This path is first and foremost a process of making things conscious. This self-awareness unifies you and unifies the split in you. It also unifies the conflicts in you and establishes your sense of self and your knowledge that the universe with all its bliss is yours. (Pathwork, 24 Sep 71)

The most blatant false search for the 'now point' is through drugs. Indeed, the drug experience removes the physical, three-dimensional boundaries and thus reveals the reality behind the great curtain. But when this revelation occurs without earning it by making the state of consciousness compatible with this experience, then the price is high. (Pathwork, 14 Nov 73)

In therapy using massive doses of LSD, a condition of chemically enforced insanity takes place. By insanity, I mean a situation in which the conscious mind is forced into a state of powerlessness. There is a literal assault made not only upon the psyche, but upon the organizational framework that makes it possible for you to exist rationally in the world that you know... Under such enforced conditions, you are literally facing egotistical consciousness with its own death in an encounter that need not occur... Consciousness finds itself in a crisis situation... because it is forced to fight on a battleground for which it was never designed and cannot understand, where basically counted-upon allies of association, memory and organization, and all the powers of the inner self, are suddenly turned into enemies. It is made vulnerable to all those forces it was meant to lead, while being stripped of its natural logical abilities – indeed, of its very sense of identity... I am quite aware of the distorted religious connections made here: Die to yourself and you will be reborn... What you think of as the self dies and is reborn constantly, as the cells of your body do... Change flexibly with the gracious dance of all being that is reflected in the universe of the body and mind. This does not include the crucifixion of the ego... There is... no magic therapy – only an understanding of your own great creativity, and the knowledge that you yourself make your world. (Seth, *NPR*, chapter 10)

You often *avoid* this natural treatment, however, and run from frightening conscious thoughts that would in their turn lead you to the source of 'negative' beliefs, where they could be faced; you could travel through them, so to speak, into feelings of joy and victory. Instead, for example, many of you accept the way of drugs, where such feelings and thoughts are thrust upon you, or forced out of you, while you are denied the stabilizing comforts of the conscious mind. (Seth, *NPR*, chapter 10)

YOUR OWN DREAM STATE IS THE MOST EFFECTIVE THERAPY OF ALL

Seth in particular also discusses the dream state in some detail, and in my view this is fundamental to the current discussion. First of all he eschews standardised dream interpretations, insisting that we each need to develop the ability to interpret our *own* dreams because we're so unique. He then emphasises the therapeutic benefits that such interpretation can have and, going further, recommends the active pursuit of becoming conscious in our dreams. In this he was foreshadowing the great popularity of what's commonly referred to as 'lucid dreaming', which in its own right overlaps considerably with – and can act as a precursor to – the out-of-body experience.

One particular piece of advice he gives is to set the intention before sleep of solving any specific problems we might face. But he also suggests that in our dreams we try out alternative courses of action. So, although we're jumping ahead somewhat to the next chapter, by extension this implies that before sleep we can set an intention to realise a particular outcome we desire while in our dream state, which should then help it to materialise in the physical.

key quotes

Dreams are one of your greatest natural therapies, and one of your most effective assets as connectors between the interior and exterior universes. Usually they are not analyzed according to your [own] current beliefs. You have been taught to interpret them along the lines of very ritualized procedures. You are told, for instance, that certain objects or images in your dreams have a definite meaning – not necessarily your own, but following whatever psychological, mystical or religious school of thought in which you happen to be interested. Some of these systems do touch upon legitimate portions of reality, but they all overlook the great individualistic and highly private nature of your dreams, and the fact that you create your own reality... Your own knowledge of dream symbols and their personal meaning is so opaque simply because you are not used to examining them with your conscious mind. You have been taught that it cannot understand. The great interconnections between waking and dreaming experience then escape you. You do not realize the many physical problems that are solved for you, and by you, in your dreams. This happens very frequently when you consciously set the problem before yourself, state it clearly, and then drift into sleep. The same thing happens, however, even without such a conscious set. Dreams give you all kinds of information concerning the state of your body, the world at large, and the probable exterior conditions that your present beliefs will bring about. The dream state provides you with a trial framework in which you explore probable actions and decide upon the ones you want to physically materialize. Not only nightmares, as mentioned earlier, but many other dreams follow rhythms of a therapeutic nature far more effectively than any that are drug-induced... I merely want to point out some of the natural doorways to self-illumination and states of grace. These can be alternative courses to those who believe that there is no other way but to browbeat the ego – either through the use of chemicals or by other methods calculated to strip it of its powers at least momentarily, rather than teaching it to use those great abilities of assimilation that it does possess. (Seth, *NPR*, chapter 10)

I suggest a six-hour sleeping block of time at one session, and no more. If you still feel the need for a greater amount of rest, then a two-hour-at-the-most nap can be added. Many will find that a five-hour steady sleeping period is quite sufficient, with a nap as required. A four-hour block is ideal, however, reinforced by whatever nap feels natural. In such circumstances, there are not the great artificial divisions created between the two states of consciousness. The conscious mind is better able to remember and assimilate its dreaming experience, and in dreams the self can use its waking experience more efficiently... When you find yourself as alert, responsive, and intellectual in the dream state as you are in waking life, it becomes impossible to operate within the old framework... A certain beneficial and natural situation is arrived at, in which the conscious and unconscious minds meet. This occurs spontaneously whatever your sleep patterns, but is very brief and seldom remembered. (Seth, *NPR*, chapter 13)

In dreams you often do work quite as valid as any performed in the day, and in the dream state you meet and interact with your own reincarnational selves... In the dreaming condition there is a great interchange of information with these other portions of your selves. (Seth, *NPR*, chapter 19)

It is quite possible to take your normally conscious 'I' into the dream state, to your advantage... Such a procedure can bring you in contact with wisdom you have been denying yourself, help unify your entire life situation, and release your energy for practical everyday purposes. Even the decision to *try* such a venture is beneficial, since it automatically presupposes a flexibility of attitude on the part of the conscious self... By suggesting before sleep that solutions to problems be given you, you automatically begin to utilize your dream knowledge to a greater extent, and to open the doors to your own greater creativity. (Seth, *NPR*, chapter 20)

you don't have to create
the life you desire...

it already exists among
infinite possibilities

Let's finally turn to the *proactive*, *deliberate* or *conscious* creation of specific goals, or desirable outcomes, in various areas of life.

We begin with the idea – mentioned briefly in the Preface and explored in detail in *Supersoul* – that each of the myriad universes supersouls have created for themselves to play in is effectively a digital simulation or, in simple parlance, something akin to a computer game. Human life on planet earth happens to be just one of these, although there are probably many different versions even of this.

We should be clear at this point that we're not talking about the somewhat nightmarish scenario of *The Matrix* films, in which the dumb participants in the earth experiment are mere pawns being manipulated by a higher intelligence. The idea of a simulation doesn't have to involve manipulation or make our experience any less real and valid, but it does provide some important context within which to view our creative powers. The key point is that in a simulation more or less all the potential avenues for the future are worked out, based on the different possible decisions those involved can make. Each of these possible scenarios is then held in a database, each one carrying a different probability based on past behaviour. Of course this idea still involves some sense of past and future, but let's leave that to one side for now.

Whether or not they go as far as to accept the idea of a fundamentally digital reality – and only Walsch's God does so explicitly – the majority of our sources reflect the general view that any future we desire *already exists*, at least as a potentiality. All we have to do, then, is align our vibrations to it using our focus, imagination and emotion, then attract and allow it into our experience using our ongoing beliefs, thoughts and actions.

key quotes

Explore. Find out what you believe, find out what kind of definitions you have about reality, and rewrite them, reinvent them, redefine them, be creative, use your imagination. That's what it's for. (Bashar, *Fundamentals*)

You may be altering *any* choices and *any* probabilities within *any* moment. (Elias, 19 Jul 99)

There is no state of being, no experience, no situation, no concept, no feeling, no object, no manifestation – in whatever variety or type of degree – that does not already exist. It exists as a potentiality, and already in the potential lies the finished product... Nothing is created anew, all exists already. It exists on another level of being, of experience, of consciousness. It can be found right now, immediately, if and when specific obstructions are eliminated... When you know something you wish to bring about exists in principle, you have made the first step toward its realization. (Pathwork, 10 Nov 67)

There are in your terms, then, unlimited probable future events for which you are now setting groundworks. The nature of the thoughts and feelings you originate and those that you habitually or characteristically receive set a pattern, so you will choose from those probable futures those events that will physically become your experience. (Seth, *SS*, chapter 16)

You, as a personality, regardless of your health, wealth or circumstances, have a rich variety of probable experience from which to choose. Consciously you must realize this and seize the direction for your own life... If you are poor, you chose that reality from many probable ones that did not involve poverty – and that are still open. If you chose illness, again there is a probable reality ready for initiation in which you choose health. If you are lonely there are probable friends you refused to meet in the past, but who are readily available. In your mind, therefore, see those probable abilities or events taking place. As you do, the intensity of your desire brings them into your experience. (Seth, *NPR*, chapter 15)

Think of the cosmic wheel as that CD-ROM. All the endings already exist. The universe is just waiting to see which one you choose *this time*... Your computer disc doesn't care whether you win or not, and you can't 'hurt its feelings'. It just offers you a chance to play again. (Walsch, *CWG III*, chapter 6)

USE EMOTION WHEN AFFIRMING AND VISUALISING

In this and the following sections we'll be concentrating on those aspects of the proactive creation process that come across to me as most important, or perhaps involve different advice from different sources. But please remember this isn't supposed to be a detailed practical manual. It's primarily intended as a theoretical primer that uses cross-source confirmation to encourage further practical exploration.

Some of you will already have read and heard a great deal about the form of words to use in affirmations intended to bring about a specific outcome. My advice would be to try not to get too hung up about this, especially if someone tells you to *always* use a specific expression. For example some, like Walsch's God, insist that to use the word *want* is an admission of lack and will only perpetuate that lack, whereas the Abraham books use the word repeatedly with no similar caution. But it's almost certainly true that we should focus positively on what we desire, not negatively on what we don't, because any focus on the latter still involves an attraction of the undesirable outcome. What's more using the present rather than future tense, as if we already have or are the desired thing, is important. Opening phrases such as 'I *am*...', 'I *have*...', 'I *allow*...' and, perhaps best of all, 'I *decide*...' carry huge power of intent.

One area of significant dispute concerns how specific our affirmations and visualisations should be. For example the Pathwork Guide's advice is to be as flexible as possible, allowing the underlying creative process maximum scope to fulfil any given desire. This approach is normally more appropriate if we're making a major change in a major area of our life, and involves concentrating on the *what* of the desired outcome, and on the *why* we want it, rather than on exactly *how* it's to be achieved and *when*. In particular some would suggest that, in cases where the date for an outcome isn't automatically fixed, any attempt to impose a specific timescale by which it should happen will indicate that we don't really trust ourselves or the process.

But sometimes we're focusing on a particular event, perhaps something in the relatively near future, and then specifics are more appropriate. In fact in that case the common advice is not just to visualise the event, but to use *all* our senses – hearing, smell, even taste if it works for you.

Abraham probably sums this up best by suggesting we should be as specific as we can be, until the associated emotions start to become negative because we've introduced doubts about the intention we're trying to fulfil. What's more we've already seen the same source emphasising that creation exercises backed up by strong positive emotions are far, far more effective than when they're absent. So what we're aiming for is positive *feeling* at least as much as positive *thinking*, and in their books they describe various ways of creating a loving and expansive state of mind *before* starting visualisation and affirmation exercises. By contrast simple repetition of affirmations without emotion carries little creative momentum.

Meanwhile Seth advises that we should continue our affirmations even after we start to get results – to reinforce that reality, *not* because we have doubts about our ability to sustain it.

One other wonderful piece of advice I've come across separately from our sources, in Frederick Dodson's *The Reality Creation Technique*, is that *at the same time* as we're affirming and visualising we should listen carefully to any inner voice expressing its limiting beliefs and fears. For example, 'there's no way I can *really* attract such a sum of money each month', or 'I don't *really* deserve a loving partner', or 'I'll never *really* be able to achieve good health', or whatever it might be. The trick is then to ridicule the limiting belief, perhaps using a silly voice or language, as in 'Oh my God, I'm just *soooo* scared I won't be able to attract a loving partner.' Try it. The limiting belief will soon seem ridiculous and be neutralised.

key quotes

Sometimes we hear our physical friends speaking the words *want* or *desire* while at the same time feeling *doubt* or *fear* that their desire cannot be achieved. From our point of view, it is not possible to purely desire something while feeling negative emotion. (Abraham, *LOA*, part 2)

While every thought that you think has creative potential, or magnetic attracting potential, the thoughts that are thought in combination with the feeling of strong emotion are the most powerful... Before you begin this process, it is important that you be happy, for if you go there unhappy or feeling no emotion, then your work will not be of great value, for your attracting power will not be there... As you are moving around through your day... collect data and look for things that you like that you may bring into your [Creative] Workshop. (Abraham, *LOA*, part 2)

Be specific enough that you feel positive emotion, but not so specific that you begin feeling negative emotion. When you speak of *what* you want and *why* you want it, you usually feel better. However, when you speak of *what* you want and *how* it will come to you, if you do not right now see a way that it will unfold, then that specific thought will feel worse. If you speak of *who* will help it to come, *when* it will come, or *where* it will come from, and you don't have any of those answers, then those specifics are hindering more than they are helping. *It really is a matter of being as specific as you can be, while still continuing to feel good.* (Abraham, *LOA*, part 3)

Words [and thoughts] alone do not attract, but when you feel emotion when you speak, that means your vibration is strong –

and the Law of Attraction must answer those vibrations. (Abraham, *LOA*, part 2)

Have positive expectancy and yet be free from specifics and preconceived notions of how and what should happen. (Pathwork, 23 Oct 74)

You may experience spectacular results at once. But continue the exercise even if this happens. (Seth, *NPR*, chapter 16)

Your saying you *want* a thing only works to produce that precise experience – wanting – in your reality. (Walsch, *CWG I*, chapter 1)

MOVE FROM SEEING AND THINKING TO BEING, DOING AND CHOOSING

There's one particular dichotomy that represents one of the greatest challenges in conscious creation, especially when we're trying to make a major change in our life – such as moving from constant concerns about money into greater financial abundance. We've seen that our affirmations must be phrased in the present tense, as in I *am* wealthy, not I *will be* wealthy. But we've also seen that they must be absolutely believable. So how do we bridge the apparent gap between where we are now and where we want to be?

The answer is that we need to believe so much in the changes we've already set in motion that we genuinely feel and behave *as if* the desired outcome has already been achieved. This is the way we change one pattern of engrained behaviour for a new one. I particularly like the approach adopted by Walsch's God in reversing the 'have-do-be' paradigm, while a really useful tip from Seth is that we should take one symbolic action every day, however small, to reinforce our new belief.

In fact the majority of our sources stress that thoughts, affirmations and visualisations alone aren't enough. They have to be backed up by the ongoing demonstration of our change in belief, as embodied in our actions and choices.

key quotes

When you *feel* poor, you cannot attract prosperity. When you *feel* fat, you cannot attract thin. When you *feel* lonely, you cannot attract companionship – it defies the Law. Many around you want to point out 'reality' to you. They say, 'Face the facts. Look at *what-is*.' And we say to you, if you are able to see only *what-is* – then, by the Law of Attraction, you will create only more of *what-is*. You must be able to put your thoughts beyond *what-is* in order to attract something different or something more. (Abraham, *LOA*, part 3)

Thought is a mechanism to translate information. It does not create your reality. Therefore you may think, 'I am choosing not to express this belief any longer. I am choosing to express another belief.' That is thinking. That is not creating. Your evidence of what your expressed beliefs are is shown in what you do and your responses. (Elias, 7 Jun 03)

Therefore, let us say that you notice that you are concentrating upon not enough money, and you decide that you will counter this. You choose to begin generating affirmations to alter your thinking. Therefore, you choose an affirmation, perhaps 'I will be generating abundance; I am worthy of money; I want to create wealth.' You express this affirmation day after day after day, and you generate no difference in your reality and you become frustrated. Perhaps you reinforce yourself and express to yourself, 'Perhaps I have not generated the affirmations long enough, or I am not generating them enough times within my day.' Now you are expressing the affirmations twenty times within your day, you are incorporating this action for a month, and you do not view any alteration in your reality. Why? That is merely one action that you are doing. You may be saying words, but what are those words associated with? Are they present? No. Do you *feel* them? Do you *know* that, within yourself? Are you generating actions that express that knowing that you already are creating that? No. You are concentrating upon you have not enough milk, you have not enough time, you have not enough energy, you have not enough of what you want in your relationship, you do not have a relationship, or you do not have enough control of your situations or your circumstances. But you are not paying attention to any of these expressions and noticing any of these expressions of lack. (Elias, 17 Mar 07)

Whenever you believe you have not succeeded or not completed some decision fuelled by desire, it is because you were simply not wholly committed – or you decided to change your mind. (Jeshua, *WOH*, lesson 5)

Wistful, resigned daydreaming that grabs the fantasy as a substitute for drab reality is not at all what is meant here, and is really a hindrance to the proper conceiving of life's potentials. What I mean is a vigorous, active, dynamic reality concept of what is possible. (Pathwork, 10 Nov 67)

Suppose that you are unhealthy and desire health. If you understand the nature of probabilities, you will not need to *pretend* to ignore your present situation. You will recognize it instead as a probable reality that you have physically materialized. Taking that for granted, you will then begin the process necessary to bring a different probability into physical experience. You will do this by concentrating upon what you want, but feeling no conflict between that and what you have, because one will not contradict the other; each will be seen as a reflection of belief in daily life. As it took some time to build up your present [body] image with its unhealthy aspects, so it may take time to change that picture. But concentration upon the present unhealthy situation will only prolong it. Period. (Seth, *NPR*, chapter 15)

In one way or another... make one physical gesture or act that is in line with your belief or desire. Behave physically, then, at least once a day in a way that shows that you have faith in what you are doing. The act can be a very simple one. If you are lonely and feel unwanted, it can merely involve your smiling at someone else. If you are poor, it can involve such a simple thing as buying an item you want that costs two cents more than the one you would usually buy – acting on the faith, even that feebly, that the two cents will somehow be given you or come into your experience; but acting *as if* you had more than you do. In health terms, it involves conducting yourself once a day as though you were not sick. (Seth, *NPR*, chapter 15)

Most people believe if they 'have' a thing (more time, money, love – whatever), then they can finally 'do' a thing (write a book, take up a hobby, go on vacation, buy a home, undertake a relationship), which will allow them to 'be' a thing (happy, peaceful, content, or in love). In actuality, they are reversing the be-do-have paradigm. In the universe as it really is (as opposed to how you think it is), 'havingness' does not produce 'beingness', but the other way around. First you 'be' the thing called 'happy' (or 'knowing', or 'wise', or 'compassionate', or whatever), then you start 'doing' things from this place of beingness – and soon you discover that what you are doing winds up bringing you the things you've always wanted to 'have'. (Walsch, *CWG III*, chapter 1)

MOVE FROM BELIEF TO KNOWING

Most of us probably have at least one favourable thing in our life that we've always believed in, so much so that we hardly give it a thought. It might be 'I never get ill', or 'I'm good at my job and always in demand', or 'I'll never have a problem attracting a partner', or 'I've always got friends around me'. If any of these is a true, long-lasting intuition and not just a passing fancy, it almost certainly means it's a challenge *not* built into our unique identity and birth givens.

But of course our unshakeable belief in this area of our life simply *reinforces* the reality that we're not going to face said challenge. Rather than just a belief it becomes more like an inner *knowing*. So just imagine what would happen if we could bring the same certainty to other aspects of our life that aren't currently so favourable? Both Ramtha and Walsch's God focus specifically on the power of such a move from belief into deep inner knowing.

key quotes

How are your desires manifested? A desire is nothing more than the thought of fulfillment seen through an object, entity, or experience. Whatever thought of fulfillment you allow yourself to feel leaves your body through your electromagnetic field, and it goes into consciousness flow to draw to you whatever will produce the same feeling from the desire experienced in your body. The more completely and intensely that desire is felt within your body, the more complete will be its fulfillment. And the more you know with absolute certainty that your desire will be fulfilled, the quicker the manifestation, for absolute knowingness is a high frequency thought that enhances the expectancy put forth through the auric field, thus amplifying your power to manifest your desires. (Ramtha, *WB*, chapter 17)

The word 'knowing' is absolute, and it brings your desire into absoluteness. The thought of knowing, felt within your soul, manifests within your being to open your pituitary to permit greater thoughts to be received... Knowingness is not belief. Belief is conjectural; knowingness is absolute... When you believe in something, the soul understands the word believe to really mean that someone – or even your own self – is assailing you to convince you of a truth that you have no awareness or certainty of, for that truth has not become an experienced reality... As long as you believe or have faith in anything, it never will be. Knowing makes it absolute, which brings what is known into manifestation... Knowing is the door that allows the kingdom of heaven to display its abundance within the kingdom of self... The way to receive your desires is simply to know what you want and know you are worthy of getting it. Knowingness is the truth; it is the giver; it is your future. When you speak, know it is. Whatever you want, you may have by simply knowing that you are the lawgiver and that whatever you know and speak must be. (Ramtha, *WB*, chapter 19)

Affirmations do not work if they are merely statements of what you want to be true. Affirmations work only when they are statements of something you already know to be true. The best so-called affirmation is a statement of gratitude and appreciation. 'Thank you, God, for bringing me success in my life.' Now, *that* idea, thought, spoken, and acted upon, produces wonderful results – when it comes from true knowing; not from an attempt to *produce* results, but from an awareness that results have *already* been produced. (Walsch, *CWG I*, chapter 12)

You cannot fool your mind. If you are insincere, your mind knows it, and that's that. You've just ended any chance that your mind can help you in the creative process. (Walsch, *CWG III*, chapter 1)

Do not... 'try to believe' that you can do these things... Instead, move to a state of total awareness. Then belief will no longer be necessary. Complete knowing will work its wonders. (Walsch, *CWG III*, chapter 4)

BE PATIENT AND GET OUT OF THE WAY

Our sources agree that for most of us, with most desired outcomes, there'll be some delay while our new beliefs and behaviours overcome those that existed previously. So one of the hardest aspects of conscious creation is to focus as much as possible while performing creation exercises, and then to let go the rest of the time and just allow the creative process to flow and do its thing. Any ongoing worry, or even constant checking for results, will only tighten things up and cause an energetic blockage. According to most of our sources, patience and 'getting out of the way' is what allows a desired outcome to manifest.

So we simply have to 'hang loose', even when it's difficult because our goal is hugely important to us. Indeed some would suggest that what we should really be aiming for is a sense of nonattachment or detachment. That is, even if in one sense our goal is hugely important to us, we'd still be perfectly content if it *didn't* materialise. It should remain a *preference* and not a *need*. Having a strong emotional intent with respect to an outcome, and yet remaining unattached to it at the same time, is an extremely difficult balance to strike – but at least in some cases it's probably the best way to achieve success.

Several of our sources suggest other causes if a desired outcome seems to be taking a stubbornly long time to manifest – and as a rough guide we're probably talking months or years, not days or weeks. We've already seen Abraham emphasising that lack of emotion could be the problem, but they also insist that if something fails to materialise it's likely we're spending too much time thinking about the *lack* of it. By contrast Jeshua and the Pathwork Guide tend more to the view that patience can be part of our challenge. This is one of those examples where either view may be more appropriate for different people in different circumstances, and it's best to go with whichever resonates best in any given situation.

The other practical problem if an outcome is taking a particularly long time to manifest is that, although ideally we should minimise any focus on limiting beliefs, eventually we're bound to consider that there may be hidden ones blocking it that we still need to uncover. Trying to strike this balance can again be enormously difficult. All I can suggest is that we restrict any ongoing time we spend searching for further limiting beliefs to specific periods set aside for that objective alone.

key quotes

Many have experienced the discomfort of really wanting something and working very hard to try to achieve it, only to continue to hold it away because they were offering thoughts of the lack of it more predominantly than thoughts of the receiving of it. (Abraham, *LOA*, part 2)

When it comes to thoughts that you feel strong emotion about – whether it is positive emotion or negative emotion – the essence of those thoughts is being quickly manifested into your physical experience. (Abraham, *LOA*, part 3)

You have developed patterns of thinking, so you can easily fall into those old habitual patterns rather than think the new thought that is in harmony with the new desire. It is a matter of deliberately using a little strength, or as you say, willpower, and refocusing your attention in a new direction. (Abraham, *LOA*, part 3)

Action that is inspired from aligned thought is joyful action. Action that is offered from a place of contradicted thought is hard work that is not satisfying and does not yield good results. When you really feel like jumping into action, that is a clear sign that your vibration is pure and you are not offering contradictory thoughts to your own desire. When you are having a hard time making yourself do something, or when the action you offer does not produce the results you are seeking, it is always because you are offering thoughts in opposition to your desire. (Abraham, *LOA*, part 3)

It is hard for you to understand these things when you are in the middle of what seems to be two worlds: the world that you created before you understood these things that we have talked about here, and the world that you are in the process of creating now that you understand more clearly. And so, some of the things that are in your experience because of the prepaving or the prethinking of your past do not fit very well with what you *now* want. And so, we know there is a little bit of discomfort as you are in this transitional stage, but there will be less and less and less discomfort as you are clearer and clearer and clearer about what you want. Much of the clutter of past momentum is now moving from your experience. (Abraham, *LOA*, part 4)

If anything seems to be manifesting slowly for you, first of all it simply may be that that is part of your script. That is the journey you are taking. A walk from one village to the next allows a much richer experience than taking a taxi. (Jeshua, *WOK*, lesson 11)

Express your willingness to grow, to be happy, to be constructive. Do this not by willing in a tight, insistent, constricted way, but in a relaxed, confident way, contemplating that all possibilities exist as potential realities, realizable for you the moment you know and will this with all your undivided being. The power is there, it is in you. All you have to do is tap it, use it, build with your conscious mind the channels that can free it, and become very quiet and calm. Listen and tune in on it. (Pathwork, 2 Sep 69)

In reality, through functioning from your liberated centre, your innermost self, you attract all the abundance of life to you, but you do not depend on it. (Pathwork, 20 Oct 72)

Part of the creating process is the patience to let things be, learning to trust life to express back to you what you put into it. That requires waiting for the seed to grow. Do you wait in doubt? Do you wait with impatience? Do you wait in fear? Do you wait in tension? Or do you wait in quiet trust? Do you want whatever it is so badly that you create a forcing current which prohibits fulfillment because its tension and its emotional mind-content defeat creation? If the waiting is truly relaxed, you will have no doubts about the fulfillment. You know that the seed will grow into a wonderful flower… As you cramp yourself into any desire that is too strong, you close the doors to joy and relaxed inner creation. Cramp always indicates negation, doubt, a negativity that you must unearth and specifically deal with. (Pathwork, 9 Feb 73)

You, the receptacle, need to be neutral. You need to give up the strong, tight, self-willed yes or no to make way for a flexible trust to be guided by your inner God. You need to be willing, pliable, flexible, trusting, and forever ready for another turn, another change you had not contemplated. (Pathwork, 23 Oct 74)

To change the physical effect you must change the original belief – while being quite aware that for a time physical materializations of the old beliefs may still hold. If you completely understand what I am saying, however, your new beliefs will – and quickly – begin to show themselves in your experience. But you must not be concerned for their emergence, for this brings up the fear that the new ideas will not materialize , and so this negates your purpose. (Seth, *NPR*, chapter 4)

While the conscious mind is meant to direct the flow of your experience through your beliefs, and to materialize them, the actual mechanics are taken care of automatically by other portions of the self. You must indeed trust that your new beliefs will work as completely for you as your old ones. (Seth, *NPR*, chapter 11)

For five minutes only direct all of your attention toward what you want... Use all of your energy and attention. Then forget about it. Do not check to see how well it is working... Do not try to overdo this, to go through the entire day worrying about [limiting] beliefs, for example. This can only cause you to contrast what you have with what you want. (Seth, *NPR*, chapters 15–16)

DON'T SEND OUT MIXED MESSAGES

Of course we know by now that, when we're consciously trying to create a specific outcome, any beliefs contradictory to that outcome – which haven't been fully dealt with, and continue to crop up in our thoughts – will jeopardise its manifestation. But Elias takes this a step further and counsels that *any* mixed messages we send out, even in what appear to be completely unrelated areas of our life, can have a detrimental effect.

Let's say we want to manifest a new job, and we're very positive about that. But at the same time we're not entirely happy in other areas of our life. We go out for dinner with a friend and we spend the whole evening moaning how our partner isn't showing us enough love, allowing it to not only ruin our own but our friend's evening too. We've just sent out a message of frustration and lack. We might think this won't have any effect on our search for a new job as long as we stay positive about *that*, but according to Elias it will. He suggests everything is taken together and can't be separated. For example, for all we know a different attitude that night might have led to our friend suddenly remembering a key contact, which in turn might have led us to just the job we were looking for.

Meanwhile Jeshua provides a perfect example of the opposite, more desirable and expansive approach, showing how a constantly open mind and loving heart can lead to completely unexpected openings and opportunities.

key quotes

[You say] 'I want a bicycle'. Regardless of whether what you are doing seems to be associated with a bicycle or not, all that you do is interconnected. Therefore, as you are generating the action of creating a sandwich and you are expressing to yourself frustration for you are not incorporating enough roast beef to be satisfying with your sandwich, that is associated with that bicycle. The imagery may be entirely different, but that energy is expressing an energy to prevent you from materializing that bicycle. In the moment that you notice that you have not enough pieces of roast beef for your sandwich, rather than merely expressing that shockwave, notice what you expressed. You can alter that in that moment, and you can express, 'This is enough; this is satisfactory'... Regardless that there was not enough roast beef, your shockwave changes, and it influences that manifestation of that bicycle in your process. It is merely a matter of genuinely noticing and paying attention to what you are doing. (Elias, 17 Mar 07)

You go to take your car to fill up your gas tank. Because your heart is open, your mind is open... You look around you and you feel the energy of somebody at the pump on the other side of the island. Because your heart is open, you go up to them and say, 'I'm just here pumping my gas. I looked up and saw you. You've got a great smile. You've made my whole day. Thank you!' Then, a conversation is struck and it is discovered that they are looking for someone in their corporation who happens to have your skills. And you are looking for a new job. The things of the world become translated into that which supports your ever-increasing joy, success, fun, pleasure, material improvement and new friends. It supports all of it when you see through the eyes of love. (Jeshua, *WOK*, lesson 5)

LIVING DELIBERATELY ALL THE TIME

Finally we come to some excellent advice from Abraham, which is more or less implicit in most of the other sources but explicitly presented as a separate tool by them. It concerns focusing on the specific outcome we want to achieve as we approach any particular activity or event in our day, and they call it 'Segment Intending'. One might regard this as the ultimate in not sending out mixed messages because, by 'living deliberately' all the time, we never allow ourselves to slip into limitation, or even to 'chance to luck'.

key quotes

Segment Intending is the process of deliberate identification of what is specifically wanted for this moment in time. It is done with the intent of bringing forth from all of the confusion of what is considered to be your total life experience, your awareness of what you most want in this particular moment. And as you take a moment to identify what that *intention* is, you bring forth tremendous power from the universe, and all of it is funneled into this very specific moment in which you now stand. (Abraham, *LOA*, part 5)

If you want and expect to receive the subject of your intent, it will be. But if you do not take the time to establish what you want, then you are attracting, by the influence of others or by the influence of your own old habits, all sorts of things that you may or may not want... Recognize that everyone you meet is not deliberate in their intending, but know that by your deliberate intending, you will be in control of your life experience; and you will not be swept up by their confusion, or by their intent or influence. (Abraham, *LOA*, part 5)

abundance is not selfish
but our birthright...

and the key to it is
excitement and joy

Our sources are pretty much united in telling us that the whole impetus behind existence is joy and play. This is why consciousness always wants to expand itself, and why supersouls are always creating new worlds as different ways of expressing themselves – just for the hell of it, to see what'll happen, for the 'craic' as the Irish would say. As a holographic aspect of that consciousness, that's our goal too. So arguably the more we can be spontaneous, irreverent, anarchic and experimental the better – provided it's an expression of joy and underpinned by love.

That means we can forget *any* idea that in order to be spiritual, or to 'grow', we have to suffer. We tend to lead ourselves into suffering a great deal because we get so caught up in the game, and often we do learn and grow from that experience. But is that the *only* way to learn? *No!* Is it even the *best* way to learn? *No!* In fact why do we tend to assume we have to *learn* anything? Expansion is love and joy and abundance in everything, which is our natural birthright anyway, so maybe our motto should be *don't learn, just remember!*

Worse again, as Jeshua points out, as humans we have a tendency to feel that we mustn't have too much of a good thing. This may or may not be a product of the Protestant work ethic, of Catholic guilt and of other aspects of predominantly Western religious approaches of the last few thousand years. But what it usually means is that, just as we're starting to attract and enjoy the abundance we crave, we're overcome with fear that we don't deserve it and it won't last. This isn't true, of course, and this ultimate in limiting beliefs should be laughed at *long and loud*.

key quotes

Deliberately guiding your thoughts is the key to a joyful life, but a desire to feel joy is the best plan of all... because in the reaching for joy, you find the thoughts that attract the wonderful life you desire. (Abraham, *LOA*, part 2)

Take the words 'ought', 'should', 'must' and 'have to' and write them on a piece of paper. Look at them. Then light a match and light the corner of the piece of paper, and let the paper burn and dissolve to dust... Clear from your consciousness all identification with such words, for all of them are denials of reality. (Jeshua, *WOH*, lesson 2)

Begin to reawaken the childlike joy of building a castle in the sandbox. For in truth, that is all you are doing here. Consciousness is your sandbox and you are creating castles. You have simply forgotten to enjoy them... So engage in your exercises with great zeal, with great joy, and above all with great playfulness! (Jeshua, *WOH*, lesson 2)

You – each and every one of you – are made of the very substance of that overwhelming love and playfulness that has the power to create infinitely and thereby to extend creation itself! (Jeshua, *WOH*, lesson 8)

The tree of good and evil... is like holding a beautiful flower and seeing the petals and saying, 'Oh, it's so beautiful. I can't quite take it, so I think I'll prick my finger on the thorn and bring myself back down.' (Jeshua, *WOH*, lesson 8)

The universe is abundant in its joys, pleasures, and bliss. Man is supposed to experience them, not forsake them. (Pathwork, 20 Oct 72)

You do have the birthright to experience this and other fulfillments, for the universe's abundance is there for everyone. No one is excluded. (Pathwork, 9 Feb 73)

So what is God, the cause of your precious being, the wondrous life force that flows and ebbs amongst all of you, that connects and binds you together, that is the promise of life hereafter and eternities to come?.. It is the Isness that is complete and utter joy. That is your heritage and your destiny. (Ramtha, *WB*, chapter 4)

The Father has not given you or anyone else a directive as to what your life should be, save for one thing... and that is for you to be joyful, whatever joy means to you. For the happier and more joyful you are within your precious and divine self, the closer you are to being the likeness of God and in harmony with all life... What is joy? Joy is the freedom of movement without interruption. It is the freedom of expression without judgment. It is the freedom of being without fear or guilt. Joy is knowing that you are creating life on your own terms. It is the sublime movement of self allowed. That is joy. Why is joy the grandest state of being? Because when you are in a state of joy, you are in the flow of what God is, and in that flow there is no room for jealousy, anger, bitterness, or war. It is difficult to hate anyone – it is difficult to besiege anyone; it is difficult to hurt anyone – when you are in a state of joy. When you are happy and joyful, you love God seen in all things. In an exuberant state of joy, you are at peace with everything about you. When you are in joy with life, you cannot feel remorseful or insecure, fearful, angry, or lacking. In a state of joy, you are fulfilled and complete, and life, wisdom, and creativity flow like a mighty river from within your being. In a state of joy, you are inspired to the heights of greatness and the depths of feeling... How do you become joyful? By knowing that every moment of your life gives you the freedom and opportunity to express joy, if that is your desire, and by knowing there is nothing that is ever worth separating yourself from happiness and joy and God – nothing – and by loving yourself completely through and through, for you love God when you do. (Ramtha, *WB*, chapter 14)

All creativity and consciousness is born in the quality of play, as opposed to work. (Seth, *SS*, chapter 3)

The vitality of the universe is creativity and joy and love, and *that* is spirituality. (Seth, *SS*, Appendix)

You need to learn the power of thought and emotion, but this should fill you with the joy of creativity. (Seth, *SS*, Appendix)

Your life was never meant to be a struggle, and doesn't have to be, now or ever. (Walsch, *CWG III*, chapter 12)

FOLLOW YOUR BLISS

This advice will not come as news to anyone, and to some extent this section picks up from the earlier chapter where Jeshua and Seth talked about questioning all our values, and always being prepared to see something as a belief rather than a fact. This time it's Walsch's God waxing lyrical about making sure that what we do 'for a living' doesn't actually involve dying inside.

Bashar picks up on the point about emotion needing to be present when we're creating, and specifically uses the word 'excitement' as the vibration that will always tell us we're in resonance with our inner core. He also takes the reversed 'have-do-be' paradigm and emphasises that the only thing we might ever usefully want to 'be' is happy and full of joy. But, remember, when we switch this around it no longer involves the normal soul-searching of 'what will I need to *do* or *have* to make myself happy', but the much harder yet more fulfilling decision to just *be* joy and love – then everything else falls into place.

Jeshua gives similar advice but suggests we do this little by little. This should help, but we should surely be honest and admit that, as a human being, just deciding to *be* joy and love isn't easily achieved, especially if we're not in a particularly happy place to start with. Nor I suspect would any of our sources want us to feel that if we can't achieve such a state of disinterested bliss then we're some sort of failure. As Ramtha makes plain, *anything* that gives us genuine joy is fine, no matter how apparently selfish it might be, as long as it doesn't hurt anyone else or limit their joy.

So if any of us desire financial abundance, a loving relationship and family, a nice house that we're proud of, foreign holidays, nice clothes and all those typical things that most people desire, we shouldn't feel guilty. Why shouldn't we want them, especially if we've never yet had them? On the other hand if we achieve them and then find they don't make us happy, as people often do, then that's a sign to change course and follow a different path. It might be that we just need to open up to how wonderful our life already is, and how much beauty already surrounds us. But this is also the time when some people discover that service to others takes over as the greatest source of bliss, and we'll return to this shortly.

Above all we shouldn't *judge* anyone else's path to joy, and nor should we care about any judgments others make of our choices. Each of us should just focus on our own path.

key quotes

Why do you hear that 'follow your bliss' or 'act on your joy' is such an important principle?.. [Because] excitement is the physical translation of the vibrational resonance that is your true, core, natural being... If you understand that excitement is your true frequency then you will act on it without hesitation, trusting that to do so will maintain the alignment with your core and allow you to be who you are, and lead you to the next most exciting circumstance. (Bashar, *Fundamentals*)

[Be] happy because that's what you want to be, and I mean truly the vibration of happiness, not just pretending, not just covering it up with 'Oh yes, I'm v-e-r-y happy', not just in denial of things you need to feel, things you need to face, fears that you need to experience in order to integrate them, that's not what I'm talking about, I'm not talking about avoidance, I am talking about the idea of true vibrations of joy and happiness... The second, the instant, the moment you are that vibration, the reflection in your physical reality has no choice but to reflect a reality that corresponds to the vibration of your ecstasy... [But] many of you will still place a condition on your happiness even when you think you're doing it this way: 'Oh yes, all right, yes, I will be happy because I know that if I am happy, then I'll get this happy reality, then I'll get what I want, then I'll get what I desire.' If, then. If, then... In order for the principle to really work, in order for reality to reflect back to you the true reflection of your happiness, you have to be happy with no expectation that you will get a reflection back. (Bashar, *Fundamentals*)

If it is not fun, do not do it! If you are incorporating action that is pleasurable to you, you are incorporating what we would express to you as value fulfillment. Your essence does not manifest for the purpose of experience for some mystical reason! Its fullest value fulfillment is expressed through pleasure... You may experience effortlessness and a pleasurable existence if you are fulfilling your desire. This is why I say to you, if it is not fun, do not do it! (Elias, 25 Feb 96)

Become committed – fully committed – to the experience of happiness, even as you have been fully committed to unhappiness, limitation and lack. (Jeshua, *WOH*, lesson 1)

God's will for you is that you be genuinely happy through and through, content, fulfilled, at peace, empowered, capable and responsible. (Jeshua, *WOH*, lesson 5)

Service is the greatest source of joy... That is why, perhaps, one gives up a job in a corporation to go and start to make videos that can help get a good message out to the world... [or to] become a minister. Because within them the soul has said: 'All right, enough of that experience. I want greater joy. And the pathway to greater joy is to join with like minds that are creating and extending contexts in which other minds can awaken.' (Jeshua, *WOK*, lesson 11)

You are free now to create *differently*. How to do that? Do not get up out of your chair and rush about. But why not decide, right now, to experience happiness, to experience peace, and to experience the knowledge that you *are* a master. How do you do that? By *choosing* to. Simply decide right now for the next thirty seconds to be happy. And then choose another thirty seconds to be at peace... Choose now to *feel* perfect abundance and joy. And then *behave* as one who *knows* they live in abundance... *Always move toward what you enjoy. Always follow your heart*. (Jeshua, *WOK*, lesson 11)

There is no greater purpose in life than to live for the love and fulfillment of self, and that can only be achieved by participating in this life and doing those things which bring you happiness, regardless of what they are, for who shall say it is wrong or that it is not good for you? God would never say that, for he will be every direction you turn and the result of everything you experience. And don't ask others what they think. What would they know of joy when their lives have been burdened by the same limitations that have plagued yours. The Father presses joy to you. He is always there, waiting for you to open up to receive it. That is what is meant by 'Ask and you shall receive'. It is quite simple to have joy at all times. Know you are worth it. (Ramtha, *WB*, chapter 14)

What is your path in life? To always follow your feelings, to listen to the feelings within your soul and embark upon the adventures that your soul urges you to experience. Your soul, if you listen to it, will tell you what you need to experience. If you are feeling bored or have no desire to do something, it means you have already experienced it and have collected the wisdom from that adventure. But if you want to do something, that urging within your soul means you must have the experience, the virtue of it. If you abstain from it, you are only postponing the experience until another moment or another existence... Follow your heart, your dreams, your desires. Do what your soul calls you to do, whatever it is, and allow it to be finished. Then you will go on to another adventure. You will never be judged unless you accept the judgment of those around you. And if you accept their judgment, it is only your will to do so for the experience. (Ramtha, *WB*, chapter 20)

Go ahead and do what you really love to do! Do nothing else! You have so little time. How can you think of wasting a moment doing something for a *living* you don't like to do? What kind of a living is *that*? That is not a living, that is a *dying*!.. You have a *right* to your joy; children or no children; spouse or no spouse. Seek it! Find it! And you will have a joyful family, no matter how much money you make or don't make. And if they aren't joyful, and they get up and leave you, then release them with love to seek *their* joy... If 'man who supports his family, at all costs, even his own happiness' is who you are, then love your work, because it is *facilitating* your creation of a *living statement of self*. If 'woman who works at job she hates in order to meet responsibilities as she sees them' is who you are, then love, love, *love* your job, for it totally supports your self image, your self concept. Everyone can love everything the moment they understand what they are doing, and why. (Walsch, *CWG I*, chapter 12)

THERE'S MORE THAN ENOUGH FOR EVERYONE

All this talk of unrestrained abundance naturally brings us back to the last fundamental objection to the idea that we create our own reality – the notion that if we create abundance for ourselves we're being selfish, because someone else will have to lose out as a result. This tends to be the view of more altruistic people, but the resounding response from Abraham and Walsch's God is that the universe we're experiencing contains *unlimited* abundance. So there's no need to view our experience as some form of competition, and nor do we need to try to justify, or feel guilty about, any decision to attract abundance into our own life.

Wallace Wattles, who was also introduced briefly in the Preface, provides an interesting perspective on financial abundance in *The Science of Getting Rich*. He argues that we can't live a spiritual life of service to others from a position of poverty, whereas the more money we have the more time we have to help others and the more charitable works we can undertake.

On an individual basis all this is perhaps easy enough to grasp, because each of us can literally create whatever experience we want – and we'll return to this in the final chapter. It perhaps becomes harder when we apply it globally to resources like water, for instance, especially when various bodies are predicting increased scarcity in certain parts of the world due to a combination of increased human population and global warming. The argument from both of our aforementioned sources is that, just as we create individual abundance or lack, so do we collectively as a species. Indeed the implication seems to be that the more concerned humans in the West worry about shortages affecting people in other parts of the world, the more their collective focus is contributing to those shortages.

From a theoretical point of view this makes perfect sense, but I must say I struggle with it somewhat and therefore have sympathy with others who might feel the same. We'll return to this issue in the next section.

key quotes

See your world as a sort of well-stocked kitchen where every possible ingredient that has ever been pondered, considered, thought of, or wanted exists in abundant, never-ending quantity; and see yourself as the chef, soliciting forth from the shelves of your kitchen whatever ingredient, in whatever quantity, you desire. (Abraham, *LOA*, part 2)

When you are in the mode of justifying, you are in a negative mode, for you are not focused upon what you want. Instead, you are trying to convince others that it is all right for you to desire, and you need not do this. It *is* all right. (Abraham, *LOA*, part 3)

In this unlimited universe, there need be no *competition* for resources, for the resources are unlimited. You may deprive yourself of receiving them, and therefore *perceive* a shortage, but it is really of your own making. (Abraham, *LOA*, part 3)

What is difficult is when you are looking at your world as one that is not abundant – when you begin thinking in terms of how many fish there are, or when you begin thinking in terms of how much prosperity and abundance is present. For then you begin to worry about someone else wasting it or squandering it, leaving not enough for the rest, or not enough for you. When you come to understand that this universe, indeed, this physical experience in which you are participating, is abundant – and that there is not an end to that abundance – then you do not worry. You let them create and attract to *them*, while you create and attract to *you*. (Abraham, *LOA*, part 4)

There's not enough… You have this root thought about just about everything. There's not enough money, there's not enough time, there's not enough love, there's not enough food, water, compassion in the world. Whatever there is that's good, there's just *not enough*. This race consciousness on 'not-enough-ness' creates and recreates the world as you see it. (Walsch, *CWG I*, chapter 11)

[One of the 'basic wisdoms that run through the entire dialogue'] There's enough. (Walsch, *CWG III*, chapter 21)

YOU CAN'T HELP OTHERS UNTIL YOU'VE HELPED YOURSELF FIRST

I'd like now to return to the issue of loving ourselves more than anyone else. The particular point to be made here, again aimed specifically at those of a more altruistic persuasion whose focus is on service to others, is that we can't do that effectively unless and until we love ourselves first. The fact that this is imperative and not a sign of selfishness is stressed by Abraham, Ramtha and Seth. The problem, otherwise, is we'll be engaged in all sorts of projections of our own unresolved emotions, however well intentioned we are.

The other aspect of all this, which is perhaps obvious but nevertheless crucial, is that we don't help others with pity or sympathy. We help them most by helping them to help themselves, more specifically to gain control of their own lives. This might be in a metaphysical context, by gently introducing someone to the idea that they create their own reality, for example – although we should never attempt to force this onto someone who's plainly not ready to take on that responsibility. Alternatively it might be in a more practical sense – if we're talking about the Third World, for example – where ideally we aim not just to give countries aid money, but we undertake educational and other projects to help them improve and maintain their infrastructure. Maybe the same approach should be adopted with the homeless person on the street, although how many of us take the time to do anything other than give them a few coins?

One warning we regularly hear in relation to this – which I suspect we've all seen ignored by some wonderful, humane friends – is to make sure we don't emotionally take on the problems of others we're trying to help, or feel personally responsible for them. As several of our wise sources say, we love them most by allowing them the freedom to pursue the path they've chosen, without judging it or overly interfering in it.

But both Seth and Walsch's God insist that nor can we use this as an excuse to just ignore the plight of others, and glibly shrug it off as 'something they chose'. This is perhaps especially true when we come to the Third World and, to pick up from the previous section, it seems the best we can do is offer *constructive* help where possible, both in terms of in-country projects, and of not ourselves squandering what might prove to be scarce resources – albeit that that scarcity is collectively caused by humanity itself.

What probably doesn't help either us as individuals or them collectively is hand-ringing with little else to accompany it. If we decide we want to take deliberate, positive and expansive action to at least behave responsibly as an individual in terms of not wasting the planet's resources, and that decision and action makes us feel good, that's terrific. If we decide to judge others for not following our example, that doesn't help us and it won't change them. If we decide to go further and become actively involved with overseas development projects, either by fund raising, personal donation, or actually working in the relevant organisations or countries, that's terrific too. But if we merely sit around feeling guilty that's moving more towards limiting behaviour. Admittedly there's a fine balance to strike between spreading limiting guilt to others and raising awareness in a constructive way. But the key, as always, is how does what we're doing make us *feel*?

key quotes

We are often accused of teaching selfishness, and we always agree that we certainly do teach selfishness, for you cannot perceive life from any other perspective other than that of yourself... Whether you are focusing upon yourself or another, you are doing it all from your selfish vibrational viewpoint... Unless you are selfish enough to care about how you feel, and therefore direct your thoughts in such a way that you are allowing a true connection to your Inner Being, you have nothing to give another anyway. (Abraham, *LOA*, part 2)

The greatest gift you could ever give another is the gift of your expectation of their success. (Abraham, *LOA*, part 2)

You really have no other choice but to allow [others] to have whatever experience they are attracting, because you cannot think for them or vibrate for them – and therefore you cannot attract for them. (Abraham, *LOA*, part 2)

Selfish is Godish. Every moment you live for the love of this God within you – every illusion you embrace and give up, everything you do to find your joy and light – emanates from your being into consciousness flow to feed the whole of mankind. When you live wholly for the love of self – which is the love of God – then you exude God into the density of social consciousness. Then you light the way for your beloved brothers on their own paths back into self. (Ramtha, *WB*, chapter 18)

Everyone in this world, whether he is starving or crippled or a farmer or a king, has chosen his experience for the purpose of gaining from it. Only when he has learned from it and is filled with it will he go on to yet another experience, which will bring forth yet greater understanding of his innermost self. When you become a master, you can walk into the murk and mire of limited consciousness and maintain your totality because you understand the teeming masses and why they are the way they are, because once you were that way. You will allow them the freedom to be limited – which is true love. (Ramtha, *WB*, chapter 20)

You cannot say, 'The poor are poor simply because they chose poverty, and therefore there is no need for me to help them.' This attitude can easily draw poverty to you in the next experience. (Seth, *SS*, chapter 12)

Genuine self-pride is the loving recognition of your own integrity and value. True humility is based upon this affectionate regard for yourself, plus the recognition that you live in a universe in which all other beings also possess this undeniable individuality and self-worth... You must first love yourself before you love another. By accepting yourself and joyfully being what you are, you fulfil your own abilities, and your simple presence can make others happy. You cannot hate yourself and love anyone else. It is impossible. (Seth, *NPR*, chapter 21)

Why does God allow any suffering at any time?.. All life arises out of *choice*. It is not appropriate to interfere with choice, nor to question it... What *is* appropriate is to observe it, and then to do whatever might be done to assist the soul in seeking and making a *higher* choice... Know that their choice is perfect for them in this moment now – yet stand ready to assist them should the moment come when they seek a newer choice... *Allow each soul to walk its path*. (Walsch, *CWG I*, chapter 1)

Never offer the kind of help that disempowers. Never insist on offering the help you think is needed. Let the person or people in need know all that you have to give – then listen to what they want; see what they are ready to receive... Despite what you think you'd like to give, leaving them alone might be the highest gift you can offer... Completely *ignoring* the plight of another who is truly seeking your help is not the answer, for doing too little no more empowers the other than doing too much. To be of higher consciousness, you may not deliberately ignore the genuine plight of brothers or sisters, claiming that to let them 'stew in their own juice' is the highest gift you can give them. That attitude is righteousness and arrogance at the highest level. It merely allows you to justify your non-involvement. (Walsch, *CWG II*, chapter 14)

KEEPING IT SIMPLE

For all this talk of abundance, some people end up coming to the conclusion that a life of simplicity – which isn't *necessarily* one of isolation or inaction – is the path to joy that suits them best. This will tend to involve dropping the pursuit of specific desired outcomes, or at least those that are materially oriented.

Although this route won't work for everyone, Walsch's God extols it, and Jeshua suggests that many unknown masters have followed it. Ramtha recommends widespread travel, and also emphasises that we should drop all pretence that we're on some sacred mission to 'save the world' and just *live*. Meanwhile Seth, in his inimitable style, compares the unconstrained joy of a 'bar patron' with the regulated self-righteousness of a strict churchgoer.

key quotes

Masters are never found struggling to survive in something they do not like. They would frankly rather sit on a street corner asking passers-by for a nickel or two to get a cup of coffee. Meanwhile they are busy smiling and waving and blessing everyone that walks by because they would rather love than look good in the world. A master has no choice but to serve – but to serve not from duty, but from joy. For the greatest joy can be to extend the good, the holy, the beautiful. (Jeshua, *WOK*, lesson 11)

Everyone thinks that they must have an excuse for their existence. 'Ah, master,' they say unto me, 'what is my destiny here, my purpose in this life? I know there is a reason I am supposed to be here.' So I tell them, 'Life,' and they are most perplexed and unhappy, for they are waiting to hear of a very elaborate plan where they will rise above a great mount and be draped in gold, with birds singing around their head, and they shall be the salvation of humanity. (Ramtha, *WB*, chapter 14)

Do you know why some of the most enlightened entities upon your plane are bums living in 'bumdom'? Because they live in the moment and do only what they need to do in order to live and go on to the next place. So they have been many places, seen and done many things, and met many entities. Thus they have harvested great knowledge and understanding of the human spirit from many directions. They are very enlightened in their state – and very happy in their state – for they have given themselves the freedom to come and go as they choose. You say to me, 'But, master, they have no purpose'. Their purpose is to live in the moment and frolic in doing something new and adventurous whenever they feel like it... When everyone goes beyond thinking that they must do this or that – or that their destiny is this or that, and they get down to the business of being, living explicitly in the moment – they will find a grander happiness and a greater freedom than they have ever known before, a release into life and how it should truly be lived. (Ramtha, *WB*, chapter 14)

This life, regardless of all the things that have occurred in your history as mankind, is really quite superb. Unfortunately, those who dwell in cities – amidst the stagnation and thickness of social consciousness – think that this is a miserable, wretched place to live. But if you ever find the courage within your being to get away from ideals and intimidation and the limited consciousness of man and go live in the wilderness – at one with the God within you – you will find that life is really quite splendid, that it is an ongoing, unlimited, beautiful thing. The reason you have come back here is to live. But you have not broken away from the things that bind you to this plane so that you can experience the majesty of God and life. You have not walked on a glacier, or hidden under a rock bridge, or peered out a window in winter to see a redbird sitting there, brilliant against the snow. Nor have you been in deep caverns, or walked in the desert and watched a snake in its quest for food. And you haven't slept in a great pyramid all alone, or gone on explorations where no one has ever been. And there are many of those places. You haven't sailed a great ocean and watched great fish jump, or followed a deer into a dappled wood. You have not done many things that are electrifying and thrilling and wonderful to your being. And not one of them would ever care about your labor, or your schooling, or your status, or the age of your automachine. (Ramtha, *WB*, chapter 16)

Many churchgoers who consider themselves quite religious do not understand the nature of love or affirmation as much as some bar patrons, who celebrate the nature of their bodies and enjoy the spontaneous transcendence as they let themselves go with the motion of their beings. (Seth, *NPR*, chapter 21)

True masters are those who have chosen to make a life, rather than a living. From a certain state of being will spring a life so rich, so full, so magnificent, and so rewarding, that worldly goods and worldly success will be of no concern to you. (Walsch, *CWG I*, chapter 12)

SURRENDERING TO LOVE

We've seen that we need to love ourselves first, and also that it's perfectly reasonable – in fact we're encouraged – to devote our lives to the pursuit of love and joy. But I'd like to close this chapter by taking this idea a little further based on advice from Jeshua in particular, whose *Way of Knowing* culminates in the potential surrender of our entire lives to love.

There is a significant overlap between this and living simply as discussed in the last section, in as much as that too potentially involves abandoning the deliberate pursuit of material abundance for ourselves and those close to us. But this time we simply set the over-riding intention to just *be love*. Or, more specifically, to bring as much love into the world as we possibly can, by giving it to others and also opening ourselves up fully to *receive* it too – this latter being the vital piece of the love jigsaw that some altruistic people seem to struggle with.

When we adopt this approach, effectively we're surrendering our lives to what some would call 'God' or 'Christ' or 'Source', but what I'd suggest is our supersoul or higher self instead. Although I proposed in the Preface and first chapter that life planning and guidance are kept to a minimum in our adult lives under our new model, this is the one decision that I'd expect to lead to the higher aspects of our consciousness exerting a significant degree of influence on our experiences – by directing us towards those that will most allow us to fulfil the objective of being love as our top or only priority. Having said that these experiences will still be ultimately *attracted* by that very decision we made. In fact we could perhaps refer to this as 'superconscious' creation, recognising that we're still doing it, except from a different level of our consciousness.

This might lead us towards a change of job where, for example, we move away from the commercial world and decide to undertake healing or voluntary work, either part time or full time, as our circumstances permit. We might change where we live, or leave a long term partner or spouse. We might feel drawn to make such major changes to reflect the new us. But we don't *have* to do any of these things. We *can* stay exactly where we are, leave our external circumstances unchanged, and just alter our inner world. In fact, of course, any changes to our exterior world that aren't matched by the even more essential internal changes will come to nothing.

Indeed this path of surrender would especially involve the cultivation of healthy 'nonattachment' to possessions and even people. So, for example, even though someone following it could happily maintain a loving relationship if they chose, their joy and peace would come primarily from *within* and not *require* external supplementation. They'd see every event as neutral. They'd know that any time we make a judgment about something or someone else – no matter how wicked or wrong the behaviour might appear to be, and however righteous our own stance might seem – we're just causing our own energy and consciousness to contract rather than expand. They'd understand that the expansive path of the 'master' is one of love and only love, while anything and everything else is a product of the illusion of limitation and fear that our ego-laden, separation-fixated human minds have created for ourselves.

But we shouldn't forget that this complete surrender to love represents an exception to the general rule of learning to direct our experience from our human consciousness, in whatever way we choose and without guidance from anywhere. Nor is such conscious rather than superconscious creation in any sense an inferior option. Indeed it's a stage of evolution that the vast majority of humans still need to master.

key quotes

Far beyond the great thrill of the magic of creating events or objects in third dimensional reality are the *qualities* that you create, such as peace, unlimitedness, forgiveness, compassion and wisdom. These too are creations. (Jeshua, *WOH*, lesson 9)

For example, 'Oh, here I am answering the door. Yes, bill collector. Hi, come on in. Have a glass of water. You know you're absolutely right, I didn't pay that bill. Do you want to know why? Silly me, I've actually decided to create the experience that I'm someone who can only create lack. That's why I have no money in my chequebook. It's just the darndest thing, isn't it? Oh, very good, you're going to turn my name over to the authorities, and now I'll have no credit with anybody on the planet. Well, go ahead if it makes your day. I have other things to do. I'm busy creating a new tomorrow. And I know that everything all around me is going to be taken from me anyway since everything birthed in time ends in time. My house will be gone, my car will be gone, my clothes will be gone and my friends will be gone. Everything I've experienced in time is changing anyway, so go ahead and take it from me now. It'll just speed up the process...' Therefore... look at all that is around you, and decide what value it holds for you. Will you see it as something that you *must* have in your existence? Or will you choose to see it as something you have playfully drawn to yourself; you appreciate it and it can be gone tomorrow an your peace will not be disturbed? Which way will you view the world? (Jeshua, *WOH*, lesson 9)

All that you do, in each moment, when you dedicate yourself to love – whether you be living in a farmhouse or in a condominium in New York – adds to the field of energy being created that will one day tip the balance and dissolve *all* illusions from *all* minds... To bring about the restoration of heaven on earth... I [Jeshua] was a prototype for what is to come, an expression in space and time of what all of you are destined to be. Yet that destiny is but the *remembrance* of what you have always been beyond the veil of illusions. (Jeshua, *WOK*, lesson 10)

we've only just started to
regain a fragment...

of a creative potential beyond
our wildest dreams

The people we most admire are those who follow their dreams despite all the apparent evidence that they're not achievable. Those who conquer apparently insurmountable odds. These are the people who simply refuse to react to their environment or situation using conventional belief systems, and create different, seemingly impossible ones – then over time, with a resolute and steely determination and sense of purpose, bring them to fruition. They serve as a shining example to us, because our sources insist that the sky really *is* the limit when it comes to our creative potential. In fact the *only* thing that can restrict it is our own *lack* of belief.

key quotes

There is nothing that you desire that you cannot achieve, and there is nothing that you do not want that you cannot release from your experience. (Abraham, *LOA*, part 2)

When you understand the Laws, then you understand that it is not more difficult to create a castle than it is a button. They are equal. It is not more difficult to create $10 million than $100,000. It is the same application of the same Law to two different intentions. (Abraham, *LOA*, part 3)

We know what you are capable of, we can see more of you than you allow yourselves to see of yourselves, it is easy for us to see the idea of the totality of what you can create in your reality... However, of course, our belief in you is not the point. Your belief in yourselves is the only thing that will make a difference and create an ability for you to see for yourselves that you really are unlimited beings in the way that you were fashioned to be. (Bashar, *Fundamentals*)

Recognize that the God is self, and that this provides each of you with the ability to be manifesting *any* element that you choose within your physical reality that you desire. You hold no limits except the limitations that you place upon yourselves through the confines of your belief systems. (Elias, 19 Aug 99)

I will speak tonight about the human capacity to create, an astoundingly underestimated potentiality. Your creative ability is infinitely greater than you and your scientists, psychologists or philosophers realize. With the exception of a very few enlightened ones, most people do not know of their dormant capacity to create and recreate their lives. Some may believe in it in theory, but few have truly experienced it. (Pathwork, 9 Feb 73)

Anytime you tell someone that something is only their imagination, you are programming them into stupidity and limited creativity. And that is indeed what happens to the children on this plane – all of you. (Ramtha, *WB*, chapter 18)

The soul is an open spiritual system, a powerhouse of creativity that shoots out in all directions... While you hold limited concepts of your own reality, then you cannot practically take advantage of many abilities that are your own; and while you have a limited concept of the soul, then to some extent you cut yourself off from the source of your own being and creativity. (Seth, *SS*, chapter 6)

I close by saying, as I have said before: You are given the gift of the gods; you create your reality according to your beliefs; yours is the creative energy that makes your world; there are no limitations to the self except those you believe in. (Seth, *NPR*, chapter 22)

There is nothing you cannot be, there is nothing you cannot do. There is nothing you cannot have... For thousands of years people have disbelieved the promises of God for the most extraordinary reason: they were too good to be true. Belief in God produces belief in God's greatest gift – unconditional love, and God's greatest promise – unlimited potential. (Walsch, *CWG I*, chapter 1)

You are a being of divine proportion, knowing no limitation. (Walsch, *CWG II*, chapter 5)

YOU CAN LITERALLY MOVE MOUNTAINS

Here are sources are a little more specific about exactly what they mean when they insist that our creative potential is unlimited.

Elias in particular reminds us of the principles of modern physics whereby nothing is actually made up of solid matter – that's only how our human brains and senses of sight and touch are *trained* to perceive it. Instead everything is just energy vibrating at different frequencies, and our sources are pretty much united that for millennia many masters who've *known* this at the deepest level have been able to manipulate what appears to be 'physical' matter in extraordinary ways.

But they also stress that we're *all* potential masters, if only we'd recognise this fact. Which means that with enough belief any of us can materialise anything we want, apparently including lost limbs and doubles of ourselves, or dematerialise our own bodies – even, literally, *move mountains* if we have the monumental level of belief and faith necessary.

key quotes

If you are able to imagine it, it is not 'unrealistic'. If, from this time-space reality, you have been able to create the desire, this time-space reality has the resources to fulfill it. All that is required is your vibrational alignment with your desire. (Abraham, *LOA*, part 3)

This be the reason that I am speaking with you, for you *are* creating this shift in consciousness. You *are* moving in the direction of actualizing all of these wonders that you *now* look to and express that they be 'miracles' or 'special gifts.' They are not gifts, for no element in consciousness has given them to you. You possess them already! They are yours. They are what *you* are in your abilities, and you hold no limitations!.. All that you view as physical matter is consciousness. Do you *know* this objectively? No. You accept this as a concept objectively. You express to yourselves that you *think* this conceptually, but it is not a reality. You do not speak to your wall and *know* that it possesses consciousness. You do not view your wall as energy in motion… It appears to be solid and therefore you believe it to be solid, and your belief is stronger than your concept of your thoughts. Your sciences may express to you that your wall is comprised of particles that are continuously in motion, but… you view it to be solid and you view it to be static, and therefore it is! (Elias, 19 Aug 99)

You can achieve that place in which you hold out the palm of the hand and desire the sweetest tasting apple that has ever been created, and it will, literally, appear… When the gap between the pure desire and the manifested reflection of it is smaller and smaller, you will literally sense in the feeling body that mastery is growing. You will know that you are merely a child of god playing, without ceasing, in the sandbox of all possibilities called the mind. And that there is, literally, nothing out there that is solid, nothing out there that is unrelated to you. (Jeshua, *WOH*, lesson 12)

Do you know that if your brain were used to its full capacity, you could change your body into a wisp of light in a moment and your body would live forever? Do you know that your brain has the ability to grow a new limb if you are missing one? Fully operational, your brain has the ability to completely heal your body in a splendid moment, or to change it physically into any ideal you give it. The whole of your brain capacity is immense, yet you in your limited thinking have been able to use only one third of it. What do you think the rest of it is for, to fill up an empty hole? (Ramtha, *WB*, chapter 18)

Simultaneously you may create a 'thought-form' of yourself, identical in every respect, and this may appear in a room of a friend quite without conscious awareness. So consciousness is not limited as to the forms it can create at any given time… First of all, you must understand that no objective reality exists but that which is created by consciousness. Consciousness always creates form, and not the other way around. (Seth, *SS*, chapter 2)

If you have but the faith of a mustard seed, you shall move mountains. (Walsch, *CWG I*, chapter 1)

Jesus... understood how to manipulate energy and matter, how to rearrange it, how to redistribute it, how to utterly control it. Many masters have known this. Many know it now. You can know it. Right now. (Walsch, *CWG I*, chapter 1)

If you say that you can be anywhere you wish with the speed of your thought, and can even make yourself manifest in physical form in more than one place at any given time, then you may do that... Saints and sages of all religions have been said to have done both of these things. Does it take a very high level of belief? An *extraordinary* level of belief? The level of belief attained by one being in a thousand years? Yes. Does that mean it is impossible? No... There are those on your planet right now who have manifested many of these higher thoughts; including causing physical objects to appear and disappear, even 'living forever' in the body... and all of this, all of this, has been made possible because of their faith. Because of their knowing. Because of their immutable clarity about how things are, and how they are meant to be... In the past... you have called the events miracles and have made the people saints and saviors, yet they are no more saints and saviors than you. For you are all saints and saviors. *Which is the very message they have been bringing you.* (Walsch, *CWG III*, chapter 4)

EVEN GETTING OLDER IS JUST A BELIEF

One of my favourite suggestions from several sources is that you can slow down, perhaps even reverse, the biological ageing process – simply by not accepting the cultural and scientific norm that as you get older you become more infirm. Indeed, according to Ramtha and Walsch's God, even *physical* immortality may be not quite as far fetched as we might have assumed.

key quotes

No one has to die. You will die only if you believe you will. But the body need not ever die. The Gods who designed it did not design it to last for only a fleeting moment in time. They designed the body to live off its glands, not its organs. And through a flow of hormones from the glands, the body was designed to live hundreds of thousands of years and never grow old. That was how it was programmed in its cellular structures. Only a short time ago in your history, entities lived to be thousands of years old... You have the power right within you, right where you are, to reverse the age of your embodiment back into youth and to live on and on and on. How? Simply through your attitude. If you do not want the body to age and die, change your attitude. Let your attitude say that the body will live forever, and so it will. Remove all things from your life that acknowledge the ending of it, and it will never end. Never have the word 'old' in your vocabulary and understanding. Have 'forever' in your understanding. Cease the celebration of your birthdays, for that only gives credence to the ageing process. If it pleases you to acknowledge your birth, do so, but reverse the count of your years and become younger. When you do not expect your death, you will never know it. Always live in the present. Never acknowledge any future other than this Now. Your Now will be eternity if you permit it to be so. Never contemplate how long you are going to live, for you will always live. Contemplate the foreverness of your body, and so it will become. That is simply how it is. Love yourself. Bless your body. Speak to your soul, which is the lord of your being, and command it to bring forth the enzymes of youth, and it will. Know that the body can live forever. And how does it live forever? By you telling it to. (Ramtha, *WB*, chapter 7)

Your own conclusions about age become fact in your experience. In line with them, if you could convince yourself that you were ten years younger, or ten years older, then it would be faithfully reflected in your personal environment. (Seth, *NPR*, chapter 15)

Do you really think the best God could do... was a body that could make it 60, 70, maybe 80 years before falling apart? I designed your magnificent body to last forever!.. *You were not meant to ever die*. (Walsch, *CWG I*, chapter 13)

WE ARE THE CREATOR GODS!

If we really are that unlimited in our creative potential, the implication must surely be that we're all truly divine. This is exactly what our sources tell us, with Ramtha especially waxing so lyrical on the subject that a number of his wonderful quotes are included.

This is, also, exactly the principle behind the concept of the supersoul developed in the companion volume of that name, using a combination of channelled material and research by modern out-of-body explorers. This was introduced briefly in the Preface, but at this point it might be an idea to reproduce the full definition:

> A supersoul is a grouping of hundreds, maybe thousands, of souls. Myriads of supersouls are projecting individual soul aspects of themselves into this and myriad other realities, meaning they are very far from the ultimate consciousness. Yet to be fully connected to your supersoul is to have boundless wisdom and creative power, and as a full holographic representation of it you are already more divine than you can hope to conceive – divine enough, even, to nullify further speculation about what lies beyond.

The consistent message from all sides is clear: *it's time for us to wake up from our self-imposed dream and remember just how divine we ourselves are as the creator gods of myth and legend.*

key quotes

It is our desire that you return to the understanding of the immense value that you are to All-That-Is, for you are truly on the leading edge of thought... You are not inferior beings here trying to catch up, but instead leading-edge creators with all of the resources of the universe at your disposal. (Abraham, *LOA*, part 1)

You are an infinite focus of consciousness. (Jeshua, *WOH*, lesson 2)

I come not with the wisdom that you do not already contain.... The power of a thought is the power to create universes. (Jeshua, *WOH*, lesson 9)

You have been taught that God is a singular entity who with his hands made heaven and earth and then created the living creature called man. But it is you, the possessors of divine intelligence and the freedom of will, who are the great creators of all life. It is you who created the morning sun, the evening sky, and the loveliness of all things that are. It is you indeed who created the remarkable creature called man so that you, who were brilliant lights in the void of space, could experience all the wonderment of your created forms. My beloved brothers, the understanding of who each of you are is indeed a collection of illusions you have been living for thousands of years. You are more than merely human. You are far, far greater than the limited creature called man. You are God. You always have been; you always will be. You are the great immortal creators who have been living here life after life after life to realize this grand understanding that you allowed to be taken away from you. (Ramtha, *WB*, chapter 5)

What did Yeshua teach? That he is the son of God, and indeed he is. But he also openly proclaimed that everyone is also a son of God. He taught nothing other than that. Everyone is God expressing his perfection as man. And what good would it be for the Father to have so many children who are imbeciles and only one who is perfect? It would not be a very good reflection on the Father's seed. Yeshua is your brother, not your savior. He was a man who had God within him, just as you have God within you... Through the realization that he was God living on earth, he became the savior of himself, who then taught others how to be their own salvation through the God within themselves. He taught everyone, 'What I have done, all may do, for the Father and you are one. Your kingdom is not of this place. The kingdom of heaven is within you.' And he spoke not of hell; he spoke of life and its beauty. (Ramtha, *WB*, chapter 4)

You want to see what God looks like? Go and look in a reflector. You are looking him straight in the face. (Ramtha, *WB*, chapter 5)

You create for yourselves a life of limitation by accepting limiting beliefs, which then become steadfast truths within your beings and thus the reality of your lives. You separate yourselves from life by judging all things, all people, and even yourselves. You live by a code of fashion called beauty and surround yourselves with things that permit you to be accepted by the limited consciousness of man, which accepts nothing but its own unattainable ideal... In ten and a half million years you have come from being sovereign and all-powerful entities to where you are utterly lost in matter; enslaved by your own creations of dogma, law, fashion, and tradition; separated by country, creed, sex, and race; immersed in jealousy, bitterness, guilt, and fear. You so identified yourselves with your bodies that you entrapped yourselves in survival and forgot the unseen essence that you truly are, the God within you that allows you to create your dreams however you choose... This life is all a game. It is an illusion. All of it is. But you, the players, have come to believe that it is the only reality. Yet the only reality that has ever existed and ever will exist is life, a free, ongoing essence of being that allows you to create your games however you wish to play them. When you realize that you have the power to think yourself into ignorance, disease, and death, you will also realize that you have the power to become grander simply by opening yourself up to a more unlimited thought flow, which allows you to have greater genius, greater creativity, and life forever... This life you are living is a dream – a great dream – a facade, if you will. It is thought playing with matter, and it creates deep realities that bind your emotions to this plane until you, the dreamer, wake up. (Ramtha, *WB*, chapter 5)

You, my esteemed brothers, are eminent creatures of divine proportions who hold latent within your beings the intelligence and the power to create all things, and yet you do not realize this. You are more than creatures of flesh. You are awesome entities expressing through form in order to continue the creative abilities within you... All of this plane you created. That is why reality would not be here if it weren't for the lot of you. The animals are beloved, for they have been given the breath of life through you, their creators. The flowers are beloved, for they have the patterns of your beauty in them. All life does, and it is all because of you. Who are you? You are the great Gods of light, the great creators of all life. You are the grand, infinite thought magnified and lowered into creative matter. You are God, the forever thought, experiencing the form called humanity. You are God manifested as man to continue the expansion of thought into forever. (Ramtha, *WB*, chapter 8)

Deep within you, you know that you are more than collective matter, that you are more than flesh and blood, that you are really rather divine. And you are. You are here to realize that, to embrace the divine principle that you are. (Ramtha, *WB*, chapter 9)

To this day most of you still do not know that God is you, that you possess within you the power to know and be all things. Thus you let teachers and religions and everyone else rule your life and interpret truth for you. You allow the understanding of others to complicate and clutter the simple truth that has been spoken for ages in your time, that the Father and the kingdom of heaven are indeed within you. What grander truth can be written than that? But many of you who do not know that still think you must go through dogma and certain mechanics, as it were – rituals, prayers, chants, fasts, meditations – in order to connect with God and become enlightened. Yet the more you do these things, the more you convince your soul that you are not what you are trying to become, that you are far from the love of God and the understanding you are seeking, for you are having to do arduous things in order to achieve it. (Ramtha, *WB*, chapter 15)

Do you know the difference between you and me? I know I am an unlimited God, and you don't. That is the only difference. I know I am, and you have yet to realize you are. Your society says you aren't, but what do they know? (Ramtha, *WB*, chapter 19)

You are learning to be cocreators. You are learning to be gods as you now understand the term. (Seth, *SS*, chapter 4)

This private multidimensional self, or the soul, has then an eternal validity. It is upheld, supported, maintained by the energy, the inconceivable vitality, of All That Is... It shares in those abilities that are inherent within All That Is. It must, therefore, create as it is created, for this is the great giving that is behind all dimensions of existence, the spilling-over from the fountain of All That Is. (Seth, *SS*, chapter 14)

This voice [Seth's] is only used as a symbol of the energy and the strength that is available to each of you, as you utilize those abilities that are your heritage. You should hear your own echo of my voice as a symbol of your own energy and joy. Forget the cringing selves that you sometimes are and remember, instead, the magic essence of your own being that sings even now through your fingertips. That is the reality which you are seeking. Experience it fully. Do you need an old dead thing like me to tell you what life is? I should be ashamed... Travel in peace and joy and safety, in your bodies and out. (Seth, *SS*, Appendix)

I tell you this. You are *already* a God. *You simply do not know it.* (Walsch, *CWG I*, chapter 13)

Here is the one thing you still cannot believe: *you are the Highest Source*. (Walsch, *CWG II*, chapter 18)

CONSCIOUS CREATION IS WHAT THE SHIFT IS ALL ABOUT

Finally we come to the shift in consciousness that has been talked about in spiritual circles for some decades now. Even if certain predictions about the importance of 2012 as a major turning point proved, as so often, to be somewhat wide of the mark, it would surely be short-sighted not to realise that a shift really is taking place. In fact it's almost certainly our collective belief in this idea, however it was originally seeded, that's converting it into reality.

What is the shift about? Surely more than anything it involves us remembering who we really are. All the scientific and other evidence about our creative abilities, and the way our beliefs and so on fashion our own experience – whether consciously or unconsciously – is now at our fingertips. The potential is there for us to stop using our brains in the reactive, survival mode that served us so well when we needed to be constantly on the lookout for danger. Instead we can learn to depend far less on past associations, and to switch into a more proactive, creative mode in which we're living in the present and constructing new associations as it suits us.

Perhaps, as I used to, you think all this talk of a shift is nonsense? That when you look around all you see are people increasingly caught up in the material world of money and power; in the vacuity of celebrity culture; and in wars manufactured by various religious or political elites? If so, why not try shifting your focus? I guarantee you'll start to notice a whole host of wonderful examples of the shift: a massive change in attitudes to homosexuality and race in the Western world; a huge increase in the number of people following their own spiritual path rather than orthodox religion; the regular outpouring of loving assistance to people in other parts of the world suffering from deprivation or catastrophe; the way a financial crisis can make significant numbers of people start to question, probably for the first time, what they're doing with their lives; and many, many more examples too numerous to mention. You'll even start to notice little examples of people around you being rather more spiritual than you'd given them credit for. Guess why? Because you'll be *attracting* it, based on your change of focus.

What's more, just as with our own lives, the way to make the increased love and joy and awareness of the shift spread faster and wider is for us to concentrate on all these wonderful expansive things occurring in our immediate environment, in our country and around the world, and *not* on the equally large number of examples of continuing limiting behaviour. This is *not* burying our heads in the sand. It's *choosing* how we want our world to develop, and influencing it in the most expansive way we can. Again if anyone wants to become proactively involved trying to change some of the limiting behaviour for the better, in a constructive and loving way, that's terrific. Other than that, to just dwell on the negatives does no one any good.

To close this fascinating journey let's listen to a number of our sources emphasising that reconnecting with our true creative power is, more than anything else, what the shift is all about. That's why books like this, alongside a whole host of others, and relevant courses, workshops and so on, are so important. But our sources also stress that they're only *reminding* us of something we already know deep within, and have allowed ourselves to forget.

In fact several of them describe how throughout human history certain highly spiritually aware beings – Seth calls them 'Speakers' – have deliberately incarnated to bring important ideas into the physical plane. They all lived in the full knowledge of the incredible creative power lying mostly dormant in our species, and often tried to demonstrate it to the rest of us. Jesus' apparent 'miracles' of walking on water, turning it into wine and instant healing of the sick are perhaps the most obvious example in the modern Western world, but there are many others in other cultures.

But, partly due to subsequent exploitation of their memories by those hungry for control of the masses, and partly due to simple misinterpretation, they've tended to be placed on pedestals as something ordinary humans could never aspire to be. This has repeatedly ensured that we've collectively manifested a subservience diametrically opposed to their original aims.

Maybe that's why this time a number of them have chosen to speak to us via human channels rather than incarnate and risk the same misplaced adulation. What's more we're lucky enough to live in an age of unprecedented freedom and individualism – maybe not in absolute terms yet, but certainly relative to the past – and of hitherto undreamt of global connectedness. Never before has the time been *so* ripe for us to take a massive leap forward, and enter a whole new era for the human race.

key quotes

We come forth not to alter your beliefs, but to reacquaint you with the Eternal Laws of the Universe so that you may intentionally be the creator that you have come forth to be... Since the larger part of you already knows all of this, we see our work as reminding you of what, at some level, you already know. (Abraham, *LOA*, part 1)

We recognize that your world is going through a great transformation of spirit, a great transformation of consciousness... We simply enjoy taking the time... to help you put yourselves in a state, that gets you back in touch with your true, core, essential selves, so that you can function in the way that you were designed by creation to function, and that is as a reflection of the Infinite. (Bashar, *Fundamentals*)

This is the action of this shift, to be objectively aware of your creation of your reality, and therefore allowing you a fuller expression of your creativity and more free movement through consciousness. (Elias, 23 Apr 98)

You shall be creating very differently very soon. You are stepping your toes into your ocean, embarking upon the new journey to traverse the ocean. But all you have engaged thus far are your toes and you have an immense, vast expanse in front of you to explore.

(Elias, 22 Oct 11)

I am here to remind you of a heritage which most of you forgot long, long ago… I am here to help you realize that only you through your sublime intelligence have created every reality in your life, and with that same power you have the option to create and experience any reality you desire. Many others have come to you throughout your history, and they have tried many different avenues to remind you of your greatness, your power, and the foreverness of your lives… It is time for man to live a grander understanding than that which has plagued him into dark ages, taken away his freedom, divided peoples, and caused hatred between lovers and war amongst nations. It is time for that to be finished. It is time for man to realize his divinity and immortality of being and cease groveling for survival upon this plane… As each of you realize your own worth and value and the foreverness of your life, you will add, one by one, to the consciousness of unlimited thinking, unlimited freedom, and unlimited love. Whatever you think, whatever you come to realize, lifts and expands consciousness everywhere… These times are the greatest of all times in your recorded history. (Ramtha, *WB*, chapter 1)

Consciousness on this plane is changing. The limitations of understanding which have caused man to be a beastly creature, generation after generation after generation, are being lifted to permit man to be the sublime God essence that he is. It is time to have a new learning occur, which is really not new at all. Deep within your soul, you will know what the truth is because the truth will permit you to see beyond the stagnation of dogmatic beliefs into the heaven of thought and understanding that has been there all along. As the rope is removed from around your throat, and the feelings of joy begin to surface and become eminent within your soul, you will begin to be this magnificent God that you are, in a state of being. This age of yours is ending. This has been the Age of Flesh. The new age is already on the horizon, and it is called the Age of Light, the Age of Pure Spirit, the Age of God. It is the age when man knows that all are equal and that the kingdom of heaven has always been within him. The Age of Light shall take man back into unlimited thought, back into a sublime kingdom of love and joy and freedom in being. Those who will be the new kingdom will not be the warlords and tyrants amongst men but the heralds of peace who are rising above the stagnation of limitation to say, 'I am God, and all whom I see do I love, for I am all I see and I love what I am.' Each who comes to that understanding will lift the whole of consciousness by his one solitary light. And one by one you will return to a state of unlimitedness, rich with the pearls of wisdom that will allow you to create more wisely in the eternity to come. (Ramtha, *WB*, chapter 15)

Consciousness is, among other things, a spontaneous exercise in creativity. You are learning now, in a three-dimensional context, the ways in which your emotional and psychic existence can create varieties of physical form... [In speaking about the nature of consciousness in general] I shall end up telling you much about yourself. The inner portions of your identity are already aware of much that I will tell you. Part of my purpose is to acquaint your egotistical self with knowledge that is already known to a large portion of your own consciousness, that you have long ignored. (Seth, *SS*, chapter 2)

The experiment that would transform your world would operate upon the basic idea that you create your own reality according to the nature of your beliefs, and that all existence was blessed, and that evil did not exist in it. (Seth, *SS*, chapter 11)

The Speakers were the first to impress this inner knowledge upon the physical system, to make it physically known. Sometimes only one or two Speakers were alive in several centuries. Sometimes there were many. They looked around them and knew that the world sprang from their interior reality. They told others... They realized that from their own creativity they formed idea into matter. (Seth, *SS*, chapter 17)

Christ was the symbol of man's emerging consciousness, holding within himself the knowledge of man's potential... His whole message was that the exterior world is the manifestation of the interior one, that the 'kingdom of God' is made flesh. (Seth, *NPR*, chapter 21)

channelled sources

To start with sources whose work is mainly found on-line, I had to choose the most obvious of the 258 Pathwork lectures from *www.pathwork.org/the-lectures* using their headings and also comprehensive search facilities. The following were finally used:

- 112 Humanity's Relationship to Time (1 Mar 63)
- 157 Infinite Possibilities of Experience (10 Nov 67)
- 175 Consciousness: Fascination with Creation (2 Sep 69)
- 193 Resume of the Basic Principles (24 Sep 71)
- 204 What is the Path? (20 Oct 72)
- 208 The Innate Human Capacity to Create (9 Feb 73)
- 215 Process in the Now (14 Nov 73)
- 224 Creative Emptiness (23 Oct 74).

The same is true of the Elias transcripts that can be found at *www.eliasforum.org/transcripts.html*, although I also used certain useful digests from *www.eliasforum.org/digests*, especially:

- choices/agreements
- effortlessness
- karma
- you create your reality.

In both cases the quotations used are referenced by their date. The exception to this on-line material is Bashar, whose detailed transcripts and search facilities had unfortunately been suspended at the time of writing. This forced me to concentrate on a summary at *www.bashar.org/fundamentals.html*.

The remaining sources are best served by books that compile their wisdom, as follows:

- Hicks, Esther and Jerry, *The Law of Attraction* (LOA), Hay House, 2007. Although they have produced many other books, this contains the original teachings in a single volume.

- Jeshua in communion with Jayem, *The Way of the Heart* (WOH), *The Way of Transformation* (WOT), and *The Way of Knowing* (WOK), Heartfelt Publishing PMA, 1995. The lessons were given over three years and the three volumes are published separately, although they and other related teachings come under the heading of *The Way of Mastery* or *The PathWay*. For more details see *www.wayofmastery.com*.
- Ramtha, *The White Book* (WB), JZK Publishing, 2004. This is the prime source. For more details see *www.ramtha.com*.
- Roberts, Jane, *Seth Speaks* (SS) and *The Nature of Personal Reality* (NPR), Amber-Allen, 1994. As with Abraham there are many Seth books, but the former is the first book dictated entirely by him and is arguably his 'master work', while the second also contains much that is relevant to our main theme.
- Walsch, Neale Donald, *Conversations with God: Books 1-3* (CWG I-III), Hodder and Stoughton, 1997-9. Again these are his main channelled works, although he has produced successors.

PERMISSIONS

I am greatly indebted to all the channels and their representatives for allowing me to reproduce so much of their sources' original wisdom. My particular thanks go to Maiya Champa from Amber Allen, April Rochelle from Bashar Communications, Paul Helfrich from the Elias Forum, Maya Kayukwa from Hodder and Stoughton, Mike Wright from JZK Inc., Zoe Willow from the Pathwork Foundation, and Eve Hayes from the Way of Mastery, for their assistance with permissions and copyright agreements – often under severe time pressure.

the Supersoul Series

all published by Rational Spirituality Press *www.rspress.org*
see also *www.ianlawton.com*

RESEARCH BOOKS

[Volume 1] SUPERSOUL (2013) is the main reference book for Supersoul Spirituality, containing out-of-body and channelled evidence that each and every one of us is a holographic reflection of a supersoul that has power way beyond our wildest imaginings.

[Volume 2] THE POWER OF YOU (2014) compares modern channelled wisdom from a variety of well-known sources, all emphasising that each of us is consciously or unconsciously creating every aspect of our own reality, and that this is what the current consciousness shift is all about.

[Volume 3] AFTERLIFE (2019) is a state-of-the-art, clear, reliable guide to the afterlife based on the underlying consistencies in traditional channelled material and modern out-of-body research.

SIMPLE BOOKS

SH*T DOESN'T JUST HAPPEN!! (2016) introduces Supersoul Spirituality by explaining how and why we ourselves create or attract everything we experience in our adult lives... so that we are never victims of chance, God's will, our karma or our life plans.

WHAT JESUS WAS REALLY SAYING (2016) is a fundamental reinterpretation of the Christian message that uses excerpts from the Gospels to propose that, through his supposed miracles, Jesus was trying to show us that each of us is a creator god of the highest order and can manipulate the illusion we call reality at will.

THE GOD WHO SOMETIMES SCREWED UP (2018) charts the author's progression from motorcycle and car racer, to pyramid explorer and researcher of ancient civilisations, to spiritual philosopher... with analysis and examples of how he has created or manifested all the various aspects of his life, both good and bad.

DEATH IS AN ADVENTURE!! (2019) is a simple yet essential guide to the afterlife, which answers all your questions such as why you will continue to exist, what to expect and how best to prepare. Based on evidence not belief, it describes the unlimited possibilities we have to create wondrous new experiences... as long as we have a reliable map of the territory.

the Prehistoric Truth Series

all published by Rational Spirituality Press *www.rspress.org*
see also *www.ianlawton.com*

[Volume 1] GIZA: THE TRUTH (2020) is the 20th anniversary edition of this celebrated book, which thoroughly investigates how, why and when the most famous archaeological monuments in the world were built… in the process placing grave doubt on the multitude of alternative theories that surround them.

[Volume 2] ATLANTIS: THE TRUTH (2020) is a reinterpretation of the most revered ancient texts and traditions from all around the world that postulates a forgotten, highly cultured but not technologically advanced 'golden race' who were wiped out in a global catastrophe around 13,000 years ago… with supporting geological and other evidence suggesting where, when and how this 'Atlantean' race most likely lived.

[Volume 3] MESOPOTAMIA: THE TRUTH (2020) is an investigation into what was really going on in what is perhaps the definitive cradle of civilisation, and what elements of modern living were introduced for the first time… coupled with a thorough rebuttal of alternative interpretations of its texts concerning supposed extraterrestrial visitors who genetically created humankind.

IAN LAWTON was born in 1959. Formerly an accountant, sales exec, business and IT consultant and avid bike and car racer, in his mid-thirties he changed tack completely to become a writer-researcher specialising in ancient history and, more recently, spiritual philosophy. His first two books, *Giza: The Truth* and *Genesis Unveiled*, sold over 30,000 copies worldwide.

In his *Books of the Soul Series* he originated the ideas of Rational Spirituality and of the holographic soul. But since 2013 he has been developing the more radical worldview of Supersoul Spirituality in the *Supersoul Series*. (A short film clip discussing the latter can be found at *www.ianlawton.com* and on YouTube.) In 2020 he updated and republished his earlier works on ancient history as the *Prehistoric Truth Series*.

Lightning Source UK Ltd.
Milton Keynes UK
UKHW020636190321
380637UK00011B/628

9 780957 257399